ENVISIONING
ADVANCEMENT LEADERSHIP

ENVISIONING
ADVANCEMENT LEADERSHIP

Candid Stories from 10 Successful
Advancement Vice Presidents

Deborah Parker-Johnson

WASHINGTON, D.C.

© 2015 Council for Advancement and Support of Education
ISBN-10: 0-89964-447-3
ISBN-13: 978-0-89964-447-9
Printed in the United States of America

Library of Congress Cataloging-in-Publication Data

Parker-Johnson, Deborah.
    Envisioning Advancement Leadership : Candid Stories from 10 Successful Advancement Vice Presidents / Deborah Parker-Johnson.
    pages cm
    Includes bibliographical references and index.
    ISBN 978-0-89964-447-9 (pbk. : alk. paper) — ISBN 0-89964-447-3 (pbk. : alk. paper) 1. Universities and colleges—United States—Finance. 2. College administrators—United States. 3. Educational fund raising—United States. I. Title.
    LB2342.P37 2014
    378.1'06--dc23

                                                                    2014015317

Book design: O2 LAB, Inc. • o2lab.com
Art Director: Angela Carpenter Gildner
Editorial Director: Doug Goldenberg-Hart

COUNCIL FOR ADVANCEMENT
AND SUPPORT OF EDUCATION®

CASE
1307 New York Avenue, NW
Suite 1000
Washington, DC 20005-4701

CASE Europe
3rd Floor, Paxton House
30 Artillery Lane
London E1 7LS
United Kingdom

www.case.org

CASE Asia-Pacific
Unit 05-03
Shaw Foundation
Alumni House
11 Kent Ridge Drive
Singapore 119244

CASE América Latina
Berlín 18 4to piso, Colonia Juárez
Código Postal 06600, México D.F.
Delegación Cuauhtémoc
México

✦ CONTENTS

To Tom Reardon, who made working at Harvard
both fun and full of meaning

 PREFACE

Advancement leaders bring together university supporters who are concerned with the well-being of their beloved institution. These strategists guide their organizations to raise money and communicate vision. They influence institutional culture and affect many lives.

In this exploratory study—an investigation of vice presidents' leadership visions—I do not propose a preferred or strictly bounded leadership practice. Nor do I identify a finite set of the most successful traits of an advancement leader. Instead, I offer a model to serve as a guide to explore the conundrums of nonprofit financial leadership and to stimulate further investigation of paths that might maximize the efforts of these institutional strategists. I call this model the Advancement Constellation, and it is described more fully below (see p. 2).

The complicated role of the vice president of institutional advancement is similar to that of many nonprofit leaders responsible for paving the organization's path to the future. Sometimes this role is described as a three-legged stool, where the advancement leader is responsible for managing institutional relationships, finding sources of revenue, and effectively communicating the mission of the organization. Often the people in these roles must be both the visionary and the implementer. Especially in times of economic uncertainty, financial leaders must find support to simply keep their institutions' doors open. These are not the people who scrutinize the spending; rather, advancement leaders are the strategists who ensure there is money to spend today and tomorrow.

During many years of working in Harvard's Alumni Affairs and Development organization, I directly experienced the dedication, commitment, time constraints, and quandaries of many advancement leaders. I engaged in the debates about the art and the science of advancement and participated in the movement toward quantification of success. I watched VPs expediently interlace ideas to solicit funding that opened doors enabling underprivileged students to broaden their horizons; that helped researchers create thriving, extended intellectual communities; and that allowed faculty to investigate practical solutions to economic problems. These VPs are people who care deeply about their constituencies. Their presidents rely on them to turn dreams into reality. The 24/7 nature of their jobs often means they do not have time to share their experience widely. Therefore one of this book's goals is to compile and distill the experiences of 10 VPs and their thoughts about advancement leadership in the hope that these perspectives will prove valuable to others grappling with similar tough challenges.

Success is closely linked to leadership. The participants all want to be good leaders who help their organizations achieve success. Yet it is not always clear how success should be gauged. In this book, I explore the challenges VPs face in defining and assessing success in their organizations. Is the metric simply how much money has been raised at the end of each year? Most VPs agreed that total dollars raised is one important indicator—but not the *only* indicator of success. Many vice presidents talk about fundraising being both a science and an art. Taking these subtleties into account, this book describes varying perspectives on the range of success indicators available and how those strategies relate to the health of the individual's organization. The art of fundraising relies on leaders applying assessment strategies in ways that preserve the sense of authentic commitment of constituents to "something bigger than us," as one vice president expressed it.

The field of advancement is 30 years young. In 2004, there were no credentialing programs, and more than five years later there are more than 100 institutions offering graduate studies in advancement. Scholarly literature on leadership in higher education often focuses on the president or the dean rather than the vice president of advancement. Consequently, students and professors of advancement have a dearth of contextual models and case studies. In a similar vein, advancement professionals do not have a wide array of research-based studies that explore strategic decision-making in advancement organizations. Thus they are disadvantaged when considering best practices, the well-being of their organizations, and the best uses of university resources. Another important goal of this book is to stimulate dialogue among researchers, students, professors, and practitioners that might address these questions and others:

- Does the model help the practicing VP seek new answers to old dilemmas?
- Is the student of higher education leadership better prepared to lead advancement organizations as a result of this research?
- Do the personal accounts of real people enliven the teaching of advancement leadership?
- Are other researchers motivated to more deeply explore coaching practices in advancement organizations or address the inadequacies of the current advancement assessment strategies?

I hope this study, which began for me as a personal quest to deepen my understanding of the connections between leadership, success, and organizational well-being, will benefit the participants of the study, students of higher education leadership, fellow researchers, and others devoted to philanthropic endeavors.

✳ ACKNOWLEDGMENTS

Many professors and students at Harvard's Graduate School of Education made it possible for me to do this study. The depth of caring and intellectual curiosity about what makes education work permeates the people and places of HGSE. I am grateful for the opportunity to participate in such a stimulating environment.

I am deeply indebted to Helen Haste, HGSE visiting professor of education, for believing that a non-degree student truly wanted to learn qualitative research techniques and commit to finishing a lengthy project. Over the last several years, Helen's instruction, insights, prodding, and support were instrumental in my completing this study.

Eileen McGowan and Deborah Garson welcomed me into their class S553—Researching and Writing a Literature Review—and pushed me to clarify my thinking. They graciously and wonderfully critiqued multiple drafts. All of my S553 classmates—Katie, Anita, Lesley, Emmanuel, Rachel, Matthias, and Honey—asked great questions and helped me make the words on the page represent the ideas in my head.

Thank you, Kay, Joy, and Brian, for helping me see where this reached you and where it needed more work. Finally, thank you, Paul, for the first and last reading ... and for all of your encouragement along the way.

 INTRODUCTION

THE ADVANCEMENT
CONSTELLATION

The advancement leader's job is to envision the heart and soul of the institution. In colleges and universities, advancement vice presidents deftly interlace ideas from faculty, administrators, alumni, students, and donors to solicit funding to open college doors to underprivileged students. Sean, a vice president we meet later in this work, tells the story of coordinating the university president, board of trustees, and one unlikely donor to provide four years of college to dozens of students from low-income families. Increased financial aid is just one possible outcome of the commitment and dedication of these nonprofit leaders.

The institutional advancement vice president connects supporters to the mission of the university through donations of ideas as well as money. These strategic leaders advance the capabilities of some of our most vital engines for improving the world at large—whether the engine is a university or a nonprofit community organization.

To understand perspectives on leadership, success, and the well-being of organizations, I interviewed 10 advancement vice presidents of a highly respected university cohort group in the summer of 2006 and analyzed the resulting data using qualitative research methodologies. I thought I would find best leadership practices. Instead I found that successful vice presidents exercise leadership in alignment with their particular institutions and particular challenges. *Envisioning Advancement Leadership* describes a framework—the Advancement Constellation—intended to stimulate readers to examine their own and others' theories of nonprofit leadership practices.

UNDERSTANDING THE ADVANCEMENT CONSTELLATION

How do advancement professionals envision leadership? Succinctly stated, a VP's vision of leadership and institutional vantage point dynamically interacts with his or her definition of and approach to significant challenges. The Advancement Constellation (see figure 1) highlights vision, vantage point, challenges, and dynamism. The first three translate nicely to a two-dimensional drawing. However, the dynamic aspect of the constellation works best if you imagine moving parts.

As mentioned above, I do not offer a preferred or strictly bounded leadership practice. Instead I use the stories of 10 highly regarded university vice presidents to demonstrate the value of coherently defining mission, management, organization, and relationship-to-president. In the diagram of the Advancement Constellation, I term this coherent definition one's *vision of leadership.*

Closely related to vision is *vantage point,* which is based on geographic location, timing, and other external factors. In the Constellation, vantage point is symbolized by the person who is contemplating the stars while standing on four dynamically linked cornerstones. Just as we each see slightly different pictures when we look into the night sky, each vice president experiences his or her institutional environment from different vantage points. Half of the vice presidents I interviewed are men and half are women. Only one of the 10 was "inherited" by the president of the institution rather than specifically recruited by the president. At the time of the interviews, four of them were responsible for alumni affairs in addition to fundraising. Alumni bodies ranged in size from a low of 60,000 to a high of 250,000 members. In fiscal year 2006, reported fundraising dollars at the VPs' institutions ranged from a low of $87 million to a high of nearly $600 million. Each of these external factors helps to create a slightly different vantage point. In the world of philanthropy, many consider these institutions (and their advancement leaders) to be models of great fundraising organizations. Since the anonymous design of the work presented in this book precludes describing more specific details of these doctorate-granting institutions, I rely on two essential premises from my research:[1] first, vantage point is critical in the study of leadership (Bolman and Deal 2003; Dill and Fullagar 1987), and second, complex organizations—replete with moving parts—demand a multifaceted examination of the dynamics of leadership (Bennis and Nanus 2003; Heifetz 1994; Peterson and Mets 1987; Wheatley 2006; Williams 2005).

FIGURE 1. The Advancement Constellation

Dynamic interaction argument

VP's vision of leadership and institutional environment dynamically interacts with his or her definition and approach to significant challenges

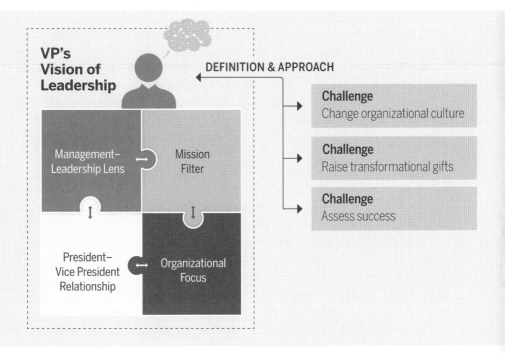

Although the institutional environments vary and defy the application of best practices in cookie-cutter fashion, the vice presidents do face common obstacles. I found three shared and difficult challenges: changing the organization's culture, developing strategies for raising the largest gifts, and defining methods for assessing success.

The Advancement Constellation characterizes a participant's leadership vision as being built on four cornerstones: (1) management-leadership lens, (2) mission filter, (3) president/vice president relationship, and (4) organizational focus. The interlocking puzzle shapes of the cornerstones represent the variations in approach to leadership. As indicated by the small bi-directional arrows, the cornerstones interrelate to form the VP's unique perspective on leadership in the complex world of higher education.

Just as the vice president affects the institution, so the institution's particular characteristics affect the vice president. The porous outline around the "Vice President's Vision of Leadership" signifies the interaction between VPs' perspectives and their institutional environments. The diagram's lightly shaded background denotes the institutional environment that forms the participant's decision-making landscape.

The Advancement Constellation depicts challenges set within a participant's landscape: each challenge is different, yet the participants see all three as significant quandaries. The vibrant nature of the Advancement Constellation is best understood by exploring the interaction of a vice president's leadership vision, institutional vantage point, and particular challenge. The bi-directional arrows indicate that the challenges affect the vice president, and the vice president shapes the challenges.

If one imagines the VP's leadership vision as a finely crafted boat, then one escapes from the two-dimensional bonds of the diagram to envision action at a particular point in time. In this metaphor, each VP constructs his or her leadership sailboat with shared characteristics and with customized features. Continuing the analogy, we envision the VPs sharing a common challenge of sailing around the world. Like the shared advancement challenges, the journey offers each VP the opportunity to circumnavigate via a unique path yet still encounter some common difficulties. How each VP's sailboat handles the unexpected storm varies, just as how each VP's approach to changing organizational culture varies. The sailboat metaphor brings to life the commonalities and variations in the challenges relative to the construction of the particular leadership vision and the given institutional seascape.

This book is divided into four chapters: recognizing the cornerstones of advancement leadership, matching perspective appropriately with challenge, advising prospective advancement leaders, and applying the Advancement Constellation. Each chapter builds on the previous one, yet each chapter is intended to stand on its own as well. A student seeking to better understand the principles essential to advancement leadership might want to concentrate on the four cornerstones described in chapter 1, whereas the new VP who is grappling with the challenge of fitting his leadership vision to his institution's particular culture might want to jump to chapter 2. However, the seasoned advancement leader might want to consider the advice that the 10 VPs provide in chapter 3. Throughout the work, you hear the participants—their voices, their wisdom, their passion for higher education, and their strong dedication to their work.

Chapter 1: Recognizing the Cornerstones of Advancement Leadership

The opening section introduces the 10 VPs who participated and explores each of the cornerstones depicted in the Advancement Constellation diagram (see p. 3). In this chapter, I articulate the participants' leadership theories by describing the tension between the concepts of "management" and "leadership"; by examining the importance of "mission" to each participant's view of leadership; by probing their thoughts on leadership vis-à-vis university presidents; and, finally, by investigating assumptions embedded in their choices of organizational focus.

Chapter 1 provides a strong foundation for understanding how each participant enacts his or her vision of leadership when approaching challenges that don't have easy answers. The quotations from the participating vice presidents serve to explain each of the cornerstones of the framework and to provide insights for readers asking similar leadership questions.

Chapter 2: Fitting Vantage Point with Challenge

Through exploration of participants' candid descriptions of some of advancement's most pressing issues, chapter 2 demonstrates that best practices do not apply in a prescriptive manner across diverse vantage points. Instead, each individual and context produces an integrated construction appropriate to the institution, the challenge, and the snapshot in time. Fit is critical. Chapter 2 concludes with a discussion of the model's implications for advancement leaders, their organizations, and their success.

This chapter shows how the VPs help institutions dream big dreams and how they advocate for institutional strategic direction and plan ways to ensure that the institution's future is funded. The chapter uses concrete participant examples to show the value of investigating advancement leadership practices by looking at the dynamic interaction of participant leadership vision, advancement landscape, and challenge.

Chapter 3: Advising Prospective Advancement Leaders

This chapter gives the reader the rare and valuable opportunity to hear advice from vice presidents who lead advancement at 10 of our country's most highly rated universities. Weaving together the dynamic interaction argument from the Constellation and the participants' collective wisdom suggests that a practicing leader should make time to step outside his or her leadership vision, institutional vantage point, and challenge to consider each from different angles. Leveraging the insights and approaches of the VPs is best done if it is absorbed with a strong dose of self-reflection.

Chapter 4: Applying the Advancement Constellation

How does a current vice president of advancement make use of this work? How is it applicable to the new university president? Can a school's dean successfully apply the Advancement Constellation? How can the ambitious advancement professional leverage this model to envision a career path? Chapter 4 maps out how various advancement professionals, would-be advancement professionals, faculty teaching philanthropy courses, and others interested in nonprofit leadership might apply the Advancement Constellation.

Conclusion

Many people concerned with the well-being of a beloved institution turn to its leaders to build a path to the future. By focusing on the person in each institution who has the broadest span of responsibility for the success and the well-being of the advancement organization, this study envisions advancement leadership built on four cornerstones, demonstrates how the VPs' leadership theories vary relative to each cornerstone, illustrates how varying institutional vantage points affect individual approaches to challenges, and summarizes the VPs' collective advice to practicing advancement leaders. Prospective advancement executives, nonprofit board members, volunteer campaign chairs, deans seeking advancement directors, presidents relying on advancement VPs to ensure a strong university, school superintendents seeking to understand their constituency—really, any nonprofit leader striving for success—will benefit from the intimate and candid stories of these 10 VPs set in the context of the easily accessible model.

Acknowledging complexity of advancement leadership, this work is intended for both practitioner and scholar. Faculty members sometimes consider the institution's funding department too commercial. In an era when many faculty meetings begin with "who has secured funds," this study uses rigorous qualitative research methodologies to examine advancement leadership, success, and organizational well-being. This work embraces the question of funding by using the tools of the scholar and presenting the findings as useable knowledge for a broad set of practitioners. These findings have implications for development and recruitment of nonprofit leaders, for decision making, for organizational success, for advancement assessment strategies, for best practice implementation strategies, and for scholarly investigation of this little studied arena.

Anyone seeking to consider flexible and creative approaches to advancement decision-making will benefit from the concrete model described and illustrated in this book.

NOTES

1. My in-depth review of the literature on leadership in institutional advancement resulted in limited academic research on the topic. Consequently, I broadened my search to studies of higher education presidents (Madsen 2002). Inspired by Becker's approach to identifying modules from other fields of research, I expanded my investigation to studies of leadership in business and political contexts. For the student who wants to pursue further research, endnotes throughout the document provide reference to scholars and concepts I would like to explore more extensively.

CHAPTER 1

RECOGNIZING
THE CORNERSTONES OF
ADVANCEMENT LEADERSHIP

At the heart of the Advancement Constellation is the participant's vision of leadership that rests on four cornerstones: orientation to management-leadership, interpretation of mission, relationship to president, and choice of organizational focus.

Although it is somewhat artificial to disentangle each participant's vision of leadership into these four cornerstones, the framework provides a means of grasping key concepts that interact to form a leader's vantage point in the complex environment of institutional advancement.

Building the framework begins with each participant's description of managing and leading. As you listen to their descriptions, you will hear a tension between perspectives on management and leadership. This first cornerstone forms a firm foundation for introducing the participants and for describing each of the additional cornerstones. These cornerstones—highlighted in the lower left corner of figure 1—shape the links between individual vision, context, and challenges.

FIGURE 1. The Advancement Constellation

Dynamic interaction argument
VP's vision of leadership and institutional environment dynamically interacts with his or her definition and approach to significant challenges

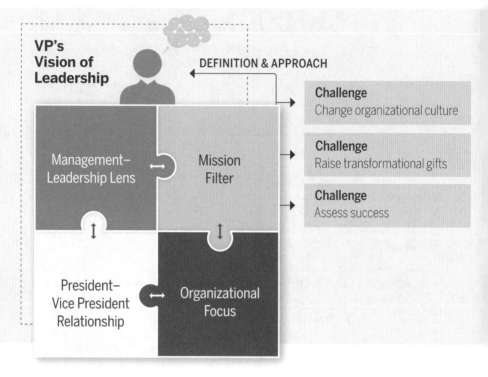

While figure 1 focuses on the cornerstones that support leadership vision, repetition of the entire Advancement Constellation model throughout this book reminds us of the interaction of a vice president's vantage point with the particulars of the decision-making landscape and the common challenges that vice presidents face.

WHAT IS THE ADVANCEMENT LANDSCAPE?

Before delving into the details of the Advancement Constellation, we need a quick image of the backdrop of the constellation: the advancement landscape. Philanthropy has been integral to U.S. universities since their inception, yet the role of vice president for institutional advancement did not emerge until the latter part of the twentieth century (Fisher and Koch 1996). At Harvard, for example, the role of vice president of alumni affairs and development was created in 1972 ("Three to Receive" 2006) and was filled by a wonderful man, Fred Glimp, who embodied the heart and the soul of the institution.

According to the Council for Advancement and Support of Education (CASE), the advancement function relies on building relationships with all of the institution's constituents, raising funds, and communicating or marketing (CASE 2012). The 10 vice presidents you will meet in this book breathe life into this definition. Each of these vice presidents reports directly to the president of the doctorate-granting university. Some oversee the departments of alumni relations and fundraising; others simply oversee the fundraising, or development, staff of the university. Their staffs range from approximately 100 people to as many as 600 people, depending on how one defines reporting relationships. Their views of who they lead vary. Throughout this work, the VPs' stories help us experience firsthand the sophistication of the advancement landscape.

Although the 10 individuals you will meet in this book are all development vice presidents, their concerns apply to other chief executives within higher education, as well as within the broader nonprofit world. At some universities, the dean and/or the chief financial officer may meet with potential donors. Executive directors of many small nonprofits act as the chief fundraiser.

Yet, connecting with donors is not the only function of advancement. The director of alumni affairs, the chair of the nonprofit's governing board, and the vice president of communication oversee other forms of connecting nondonors with each other and with a beloved institution. The goal of the connection might be to solicit help in governing the university, or it might be to get feedback on future directions, or to engage the individual in a lifelong learning opportunity. In all these cases, the overarching goal of the executive is to support the mission of the institution and to garner support through ideas as well as money.

While the role of the advancement vice president is integral to the success of most institutional presidents, this second tier of institutional leadership is not often studied. Nor, until recently, has advancement itself been a topic of study. According to M. J. Drozdowski, writing for the *Chronicle of Higher Education* (Drozdowski 2004), relatively few college or university programs focused on teaching fundraising and university development. By 2009, CASE reported 260 programs (CASE InfoCenter 2008), and this number nearly doubled by 2011 (CASE Career Central 2012). Despite this impressive progress, a great deal of room for improvement remains. Unfortunately, none of the participants of this study had the benefit of graduating from any of these new advanced-degree programs; instead, their stories reflect lessons learned through deep experience. Closely linked to the lack of focus on credentials is the lack of scholarly research on advancement leadership. The stories of these 10 advancement professionals and the corresponding research comprise a step in this direction.

Advancement is critical to many nonprofits, not just colleges and universities. Often nonprofit executive director job descriptions specifically reference the importance of managing fundraisers or leading the organization's efforts in soliciting donations. Yet these same job descriptions do not require the successful candidate to be a certified fund raising executive (CFRE). Others in nonprofit leadership roles, such as volunteer campaign chairs and foundation board chairs, are often successful business people who don't have training or experience in the role of raising funds for nonprofit missions. Clearly, the advancement landscape encompasses more arenas than higher education.

The relative newness of the profession, the lack of academic scholarship focused on exploring advancement leadership, the relative lack of credentialing programs, and the broad scope of the field combine to disadvantage many advancement leaders who break new ground as they grapple with significant decisions and transformational change. The Advancement Constellation offers a concrete and straightforward way of thinking about the complicated factors affecting an advancement leader's role—whether the particular leader's landscape is a private high school, a university, or any other important engine for good.

ARE ADVANCEMENT VICE PRESIDENTS MANAGERS OR LEADERS?

When asked this question, the VPs in this study gave answers that reflect varying perspectives and reveal distinctions in their decision making. Some were settled in their answers; others were still searching for a comfortable focal point.

Unfortunately, there is not much research on the management-leadership balancing act that many advancement vice presidents face. Much has been written about leadership in higher education, but it has been focused on the perspective of the institutional president (McLaughlin 1996, 2004; McLaughlin and Riesman 1990). Relatively little has been written from the vantage point of the second-in-command.

When one examines the comments about leadership by the vice presidents in this study (see sidebar, "Vice Presidents' Leadership Theories"), a number of similarities are evident. For example, several participants mention the importance of honesty and integrity. Others consider strategy, vision, and inspiration to be integral to leadership. While the participants seem to agree somewhat about such aspects of leadership, they appear to disagree about the degree to which *management skills* are essential to or synonymous with leadership in general and advancement leadership in particular. The participants' disagreement on the resolution of this management-leadership tension is echoed in the scholarship on both management and leadership (Bennis and Nanus 2003; Mintzberg 1990). A close examination of the main elements of each VP's vision of leadership reveals two lenses—a leadership lens and a management lens—and how these lenses intersect.

Vice Presidents' Leadership Theories[1]

PAT [A leader is] someone who has a vision of what the mission is—a clear understanding of the mission of the organization that they are running—who is committed to the organization's success over and above their own success—who is results oriented—has a clear sense of the values and principles that should guide the conduct of the organization as it strives to achieve those results. And is passionate about the goals [281–85].[2]

JORDAN So the difference between managing and leading: I have to be passionate. I have to be positive. I have to show people how we can do things. I have to lead them, encourage them and be strategic [362–64].

CHRIS But I think that the best leaders are good managers too. A good leader inspires people. Really motivates people and makes them feel really special for being part of that organization ... [a]nd really encapsulates the mission, the values, the ethics of the place [475–81].

LEE I think clarity of core values—what is important to the leader. And then the ability to articulate that drives how they do business and what they see as important [281–82].

SANDY I don't want to be presumptuous and make statements about what it means to be a good leader. I do not know whether I am a good leader or not. I can talk about what I would like to accomplish or my style [274–75]. I think the best VPs are those who see themselves in a service role and not as the big shots who are in love with their position [409–11].

ALEX It's honesty. It's integrity. It's—and by extension—a commitment to a work ethic and a commitment to the individuals and the institution. It's setting an example. It's setting the pace. ... Ultimately I think leadership is subverting your own individual agenda and supplanting it with what you believe is the right agenda for the group that you are leading [726–33].

JO I think probably leadership, like success, is to a certain extent situational. Because I think there are a lot of different ways in which people lead [537–38]. So I think that clearly—you always hear and I think it's really true that the sense of leadership—really being able to stay focused on the big picture and finding ways to inspire people to kind of lift up and do that [558–60].

SEAN The best definition of leadership that I think I ever heard and I ascribe to and try to live up to and practice is one that George C. Marshall used. He said leadership—the best kind of leadership—is the ability to get people to do better than they know how to do [597–99]. So Wills, when he is writing this book about great leaders in history, says the call of leaders is a certain trumpet—being clear, something you can understand, is predictable [1002–3].

TERRY I think the most important thing to me is integrity. ... But on the list of things that have driven me mad over the years, one could never question the integrity or the decency of the three presidents that I worked for. You know I—now—integrity is not sufficient ... but it's increasingly needed in our complicated world—seems to be of paramount importance. And you'd like someone to be visionary and inspirational and warm and fuzzy and handsome and beautiful [laughter] and sing the national anthem in four languages. I just think that integrity has got to be the very most ... [363–70].

GENE And at a certain point you want leaders who have the vision and strategy to move an organization forward, to optimize it and ... that's where they should spend most of their time and effort—the higher up they are in the organization [40–43].

Imagine that each vice president has only two lenses available—a management lens and a leadership lens. As each person approaches an institutional challenge, he or she must choose which lens to use. We gain insights into the management-leadership balancing act by looking closely at how the VPs talk about leadership, at their varying views of management vis-à-vis leadership, and where each person's comments situate him or her within the management-leadership lens.

Leadership Lens

As the VPs discuss leadership, several concepts occur throughout their comments—*inspiration, vision, strategy, commitment,* and *integrity.* In some cases the participants describe leaders as motivating, leading, or encouraging rather than inspiring. Although the terms vary, these ideas all deal with acting through another individual or group of individuals to achieve a goal, as opposed to achieving a target through a leader's own actions.

The particular choice of words suggests varying attitudes about the role of a leader. For example, *inspire* implies a slightly grander idea of the ultimate goal than does *motivate. Inspire* is from the Latin root word *spirare,* which means "to breathe," thus explaining the archaic meaning "to breathe life into" (American Heritage College Dictionary 2004).

In addition to noting which leadership concepts are essential to each participant, the use of words to convey the concepts is meaningful.

In various cases, *vision* is referenced as a plan, a road map, or the call of a trumpet. Yet in each case, the leader is portrayed as a person who sees and articulates a big picture. A leader inspires others to enact a plan or reach a goal.

Closely aligned with the concept of vision is *strategy,* or being focused on addressing large variables. Several participants' comments convey the concept of *commitment,* either through that actual word or through words such as *service, mission,* or *positive attitude.* These all convey the sense of leaders being dedicated to goals that are greater than individual personal goals. Some participants explicitly state that leaders put the institution first.

Finally, several of the participants reference the importance of leaders having *integrity*. In some cases, the concept of integrity is conveyed by the discussion of core values or ethics. Several participants speak in the first person, reflecting their assumption that the VP role is synonymous with being a leader. This implies a commonly held notion that a position of authority is indicative of a leadership position (Heifetz 1994). Not every participant mentions all of these aspects of leadership, but no one voices disagreement with any of the above qualities. Their talk of situating management in relationship to leadership does highlight differences of opinion, however, and it is these differences that seem to play an integral role in each VP's approach to key advancement challenges.

Management Lens

Several participants equate managers with leaders, while others talk about the two concepts being different in key ways. They all seem to portray managers as "doers," or functional contributors. Managers are the people who execute the vision or build the bridge envisioned by the leader. The direct quotations in the sidebar "Perspectives on the Notion of 'Manager'" represent each VP's most salient statement about managers and serve to highlight the distinctions between the perspectives.

Some of the participants reference the need for managers to address human resource issues. This is particularly relevant to an advancement office, where often the most expensive item on any VP's budget is personnel. Others suggest technical or functional expertise is critical. Some emphasize the significant role intuition plays in decision making, while others stress the importance of data. Most suggest notions of managers working within a framework or structure or set of principles. Beyond the high-level common characteristics, each participant seems to emphasize different aspects of management, but again, not necessarily ones that might cause fellow participants to object.

However, in the eyes of the VP, the extent to which management overlaps leadership seems to be a point where many of the participants demonstrate a tension in their individual comments as well as in comparison with the talk of their fellow vice presidents.

Perspectives on the Notion of "Manager"

PAT I think leadership is defining the overall strategy and the principles by which you want an organization to operate, the results that you want to achieve, and then it's putting in place a structure that will help managers work towards those results, abide by those principles, and grow [361–64].

JORDAN Great managers need to be really experts in their particular field. They need to be extremely gifted at HR issues, technical aspects of moving an organization, and the implementation of that [390–92].

CHRIS I think there are certain things that good managers have to do. One is they really have to care about their people. You have to really want them to grow and develop and all of that. In some cases, the kindest thing you can do is give tough feedback. I think good managers are also highly organized and can balance quite a number of things and can prioritize well [484–501].

LEE I think management is the execution of the vision. [pause] But my colleagues at the Business School would probably argue with that [678–79].

SANDY A good manager has to recognize who one can let loose. But a good manager also has to take responsibility and accountability to make sure that things go all right [281–82].

ALEX And then ultimately part of what managers are paid to do and part of what leadership is about at all levels is judgment [335–36]. ... You can lead people to the cliff and have them jump off and that's leadership. But to lead people to the cliff and have the manager to be there to build the bridge to the other side—that is success [755–57].

JO I think management is a hugely undervalued thing in places like universities where the key stakeholders—the faculty—are not managers [620–21].

SEAN So without the buzz words of *empowerment* and all that. I've tried to hire people that are essentially smarter than I am. [laughter] Better able to do their jobs than I would be. And to give them the support and resources they need to do the job. What I hope I can add in most cases is more experience. And kind of judgment. *Experience* is the best word. Having tried and failed things. And tried to know what works and what doesn't. That more or less has been my simplistic management philosophy [599–605].

TERRY I think that the thing that I believe is the single most important thing in—for a talented fundraiser—is the same thing that is important for a talented manager—and that is simply the ability to listen. And I think that's the most important part of relationships, whether they are with donors or they are with staff. And I think that it is a quality that not very many people have or not enough people have [684–88].

GENE A couple of levels down [from the VP]—management is an incredibly important skill [43–44]. ... For most people there are functional skills and expertise that are really important. Whether you're a member of the dining services staff and you are a pastry chef or you are a breakfast cook or you're a coach or you're a frontline fundraiser, there are some fundamental things that you need to do. And the managers need to be able to supervise that [49–50].

Tension in the Lenses

Participants revealed their views of the intersection of management with leadership during the interviews. The sidebar "Management and Leadership Intersection" captures these views. Below is my shorthand for the participant's view.

Management and Leadership Intersection
* Participant View

PAT I think the toughest transition is the one from management to leadership [351]. Moving from doing to inspiring [375].

VP is leader more than manager

JORDAN I do see them as different. I don't think that you can be a great leader—a really truly great leader and accomplish things—if you don't understand some of the basic fundamental principles of management [344–46].

Leader with management skills

CHRIS I would define it differently, although I personally think that ... great leaders need to be good managers too [473–74].

Leader and manager intertwined

LEE I think that leadership is a vision and a road map of where you want to go and how you are going to get there. I think that it has to have all of the large variables accounted for—you know, How are we going to be measured? What are the benchmarks for success? [672–74].

VP is leader

SANDY I think it's very important to develop your staff and to motivate them to do their best. I think everybody would say that [267–77].

VP is manager and leader

ALEX I think that you can be a great manager, but I think at the end of the day leadership—in addition to integrity—does require vision [744–46]. ... Leaders have to inspire. And I think people work for managers and people follow leaders [748–50].

VP is leader

JO I think so but I also think really good leaders are going to make sure that there's good management—even if they're not the ones exercising it on a day-to-day basis [619–20]. ... Or the sense about management and leadership kind of stuff and I find that that's the hardest to describe—because it's easier to describe extremes—and it's the hardest to maintain, because it almost is that feeling that any day [there are] forces pushing you in both directions and it's much easier to just go to one extreme [633–36].

Leader who relies on good managers

SEAN I haven't read 50 leadership manuals. I think there are more similarities between leadership in the military and management in the military and academia than academia would like to admit. I mean they're both organizational structures. They both have to succeed— and any leadership and management have to succeed by building some kind of consensus [605–9].

Leadership and management intertwined

TERRY I'm not a student of management and I'm not a student—in some respects—of the organization and structure of fundraising. It doesn't interest me so much. And I hate management gobbledygook [193–95].

Not using the lens

GENE Well, so I think there are big differences between management and leading [40].

Two different concepts

Let's examine these quotes and other aspects of the participants' talk to understand more about what the VPs say—and assume—about leadership.

Case 1. Pat

MANAGER   LEADER

VPs should look through a leadership lens

Pat articulates a clear, compact description of a leader. She says that she sees a difference between the lenses of manager and leader, and she separates them as two distinct states that are connected by a "transition." At one point during her interview, Pat notes that she considers this transition difficult; at other points, she says that she struggles with delegating and wants to "do" a particular task herself rather than allow someone else to either fail or provide an unsatisfactory outcome. In this way she defines the lenses as overlapping minimally. For Pat, the role of the VP is to look through the leadership lens.

Case 2. Jordan

MANAGER   LEADER

VPs are leaders with management skills

Jordan states that there is a difference between leadership and management. He portrays a good manager as someone who is a functional expert, who implements, and who addresses human resource issues. His description of the intersection implies that a leader has grown up through the ranks and appreciates the difficulties of "doing" but keeps his focus on the big picture. His definition of leadership uses "I," thus positioning the VP as a leader with management skills.

Case 3. Chris

MANAGER = LEADER

VPs are good managers and good leaders

Chris describes the best leaders as good managers. She references a former boss who encapsulated her definition of good leader and good manager. Thus, for Chris, a VP is both a good manager and a good leader.

Case 4. Lee

LEADER

VPs are leaders

According to Lee, leaders have a clear set of values and use those values to drive their actions. He says that managers implement the vision that leaders define. Lee describes his three key values early in his interview and references those frequently throughout the interview. He describes his efforts to define key variables and to measure those key variables. In this way he situates the VP as a leader.

Case 5. Sandy

MANAGER = LEADER

VPs are good managers and leaders

Sandy positions herself as a good manager who does not want to be "presumptuous" about whether she is a good leader. She equates leaders with VPs and thus ties the concept of leadership to authority and role. Like several of her colleagues, she does not distinguish between leading and managing. Thus when she talks about good management she is also referencing good leadership. She says that good managers delegate responsibly and care about the development of their staff.

Case 6. Alex

MANAGER   LEADER

Managers need to transition to leadership role

Alex talks about leadership in terms of action traits: honesty, integrity, commitment, inspiration, wisdom, modeling, vision, and judgment. He sums up his perspective through his metaphor of the manager implementing the bridge that the leader has envisioned and inspired. Like Pat, Alex says good managers need to transition to the VP leadership role.

Case 7. Jo

MANAGER   LEADER

VPs are good leaders
supported by good managers

Jo describes leaders as having a clear idea of a big picture, staying focused on that vision, and inspiring others to help enact that vision. She says that leaders need to "earn respect, build relationships, and find opportunities" [284–85] rather than command. She talks about the importance of good management—especially at a university, where academicians are often solo contributors. She says a good leader will surround herself with good managers; she situates the VP as just this—a good leader who is supported by good managers. However, she also says that leadership is situational; and as you will see in later sections, Jo enacts her definition of a good manager at times and a good leader at other times. It makes sense that she describes seeking a delicate balance between notions such as leadership and management.

Case 8. Sean

VPs are good managers and good leaders

Like several of his fellow participants, Sean merges his talk of leadership and management into one concept. Leaders and managers are both people who inspire the best in others. His stories position the VP as both a good manager and a good leader.

Case 9. Terry

Disinclined to use the management-leadership lens

Terry does not consider herself a student of management or fundraising. From her seasoned fundraising perspective, she suggests that the current breed of VPs needs to understand management principles and assessment methods more than is comfortable for her. She says that she associates quantitative assessment techniques with good management, but she notes that her intuition often gives her more reliable results than the quantitative analysis provided to her by her staff. She unequivocally states that integrity is the most critical aspect of good leadership. Her talk of leadership situates her as disinclined to use the management-leadership lens.

Case 10. Gene

VPs are leaders

Gene says that he sees a big difference between management and leadership. His choice of words suggests a continuum where "at some point" a manager transitions from being focused on his or her expertise to being focused on providing a vision and a strategy to make an organization as optimal as possible. In addition, his words imply that leading is done at the top of an organization and therefore is in some ways tied to authority. At one point he describes wanting to develop members of his staff to be leaders and talks about sending them to a top-flight business school—implying that prospective leaders need to "wrap their minds around" what it means to be a leader. Gene says he is both strategic and focused on his vision of continuous improvement of the development office; thus he situates the VP as a leader.

Management-Leadership Tension: In Summary

Each of the 10 participants has found a way to resolve the tension between the management and the leadership perspectives. By thinking about the participants' quotations in light of the management-leadership lens, the scope of the lens, and the direction of the lens, we can learn much about their leadership theories.

This examination can also provide insights for the reader. Attempting to unravel one's own conceptions of management and leadership is a good first step to situating oneself in the management-leadership lens. Knowing whether one wants to move from individual contributor role to management to leadership is an important cornerstone of formulating one's vision. As described in subsequent sections, a participant's management-leadership lens is reflected and amplified in the participant's understanding of mission, relationship to the president, relationship to donors, relationship to the development office, approach to institutional culture, approach to assessing success, and approach to large gift development strategies.

Additionally, thinking in terms of the management-leadership lens can help in the following ways:

- Understanding how a prospective candidate navigates this tension can help institutional presidents and nonprofit boards screen candidates for appropriate fit.

- Current vice presidents would be wise to mentor potential future leaders to embrace options for approaching the management-leadership tension.

HOW DO YOU DEFINE YOUR MISSION?

For-profit and nonprofit organizations alike are concerned with mission. In the world of philanthropy, one might say that raising money is the simple mission of the nonprofit advancement leader. Since all the VPs in this study perceive their mission to be to raise money, we need to go beyond that simple summary. What do the participants' thoughts about mission tell us about their perspectives on leadership?

During their interviews, the 10 VPs made four noticeable additions to the mission statement (i.e., to raise money). Each variation refines the orientation of the participant's management-leadership lens and/or highlights how the participant's mission clarifies his or her leadership theory. The four variations of the mission statement (described below) relate to institutional priorities, maximum money, long-term focus, and building relationships.

Just as a filter applied to a camera lens modifies the resulting image, the application of a mission filter to the vice president's management-leadership lens modifies the VP's approach to challenges. By keenly listening to the variations in mission, you will gain insights into each VP's leadership theory and, hopefully, stimulate your own thinking about how mission affects your leadership vision.

Let's look more closely at the four ways in which the VPs refined their mission of raising money.

1. Asserting Institutional Priorities

Many of the participants explicitly consider institutional priorities to be a critical component of raising funds and expressed concern for practices that disregard institutional priorities. A vice president's choice to talk about institutional priorities aligns the speaker with a focus on articulating goals that are important to the university and demonstrates that the speaker has vision—an aspect of the leadership portion of the lens. In a previous section, we read how several participants mentioned defining goals and creating a plan when talking about vision. So, for example, a VP who talks about fundraising that is aligned with institutional priorities makes a distinction against fundraising that has other goals and thus draws attention to an element of his or her vision of best practices.

In a similar vein, the way in which the VP describes setting university priorities helps elucidate the participant's focal point in the management-leadership lens. Some participants describe being members of a senior university team comprising deans, other vice presidents, and the president. These participants see themselves as actively helping create the vision or set the institutional priorities or lead the planning process for the university, indicating that these participants are looking through the leadership/vision part of the lens. Their sense of agency underscores that the participant is exercising vision. (In chapter 3 we'll look more closely at how the VPs apply their sense of agency, their leadership theories, and their concept of mission to tackling the challenge of building large gift strategies.)

Other participants—like Jordan—say that the university plan is crafted by the president and that they do not want to disrupt the president's good work. These participants appear to be looking through the management/function aspect of the lens. They talk about being implementers—people who build bridges envisioned by the president. When we apply the mission filter to Jordan's concept of leadership—which is related to his setting an example and inspiring others—we show the VP orienting the management-leadership lens to the situation.

Still others talk about executing a personal plan either in addition to or instead of institutional priorities. This does not seem to align with the notion of loftier goals that many of the participants discuss in conjunction with leaders who inspire people to stretch beyond preconceived ideas and personal plans. Thus the discussion of a personal plan *without* reference to the institutional plan is evidence that these VPs view the mission from more of the management aspect of the lens. Just as there is a tension between management and leadership, so there seems to be a tension between personal mission and institutional mission.

We see this tension or ambiguity in Lee's discussion of mission. For Lee, plans or "road maps" are important aspects of demonstrating the visionary part of leadership. However, Lee says that executing the vision is management, not leadership. So when Lee describes having a personal plan prior to beginning his new role as vice president, he is enacting his version of leadership. And when he talks about executing that personal plan, he is enacting his concept of management. By examining both Lee's and Jordan's comments about setting priorities, we gain a better understanding of how each enacts his form of leadership, and we see the kaleidoscope effect of layering a VP's mission filter atop the management-leadership lens.

2. Raising the Maximum Money

Pat specifically modified her mission statement with the notion of raising the *maximum* amount of money. Her specificity helps to situate her looking through the leadership/vision aspect of the lens because she is not accepting the standard mission statement or the standard set of goals. While I find it hard to imagine that any of the other participants would disagree that each should be striving to raise the maximum amount of money, only one chose to articulate what others might assume, and thus her specificity lets us see a glimmer of how her particular mission statement serves as a filter for the way that she approaches the challenge of large-gift development strategy. (We'll see in chapter 3 how Pat's mission filter, in coordination with her leadership theory, affects her large-gift development strategy.)

3. Focusing on the Long Term

Closely related to institutional priorities and to the notion of maximum dollars is the concept of time. Is the participant focusing on short-term or long-term priorities? Is the sense of raising money for the future of the university mentioned as part of the advancement mission? Several of the participants spent a great deal of energy talking about the importance of raising money for the long term. For example, a VP who includes the long term as a priority in his mission statement also struggles with how to reward staff and donors for sharing a focus on the long term. In addition to affecting the way in which participants talk about key challenges, the particular mission modification of "the long term" is associated with the idea of strategy and a focus on large variables. The vice presidents associate both of these concepts with leadership—thus situating participants who discussed long-term focus in the leadership/strategy part of the lens.

4. Building Relationships

Several participants talked about having a dual mission. In addition to mentioning fundraising, they talked about the need to engage constituents. One might think that such a modification to the mission statement would come from those participants who have "alumni relations" in their job titles; however, no such correlation exists in this group. Several participants talked about the best advancement work being done by building relationships with donors, alumni, students, and other university administrators. By examining the rationale for choosing to make this mission modification, we gain deeper insights into the participant's mission filter. For example, Sandy does not have direct responsibility for alumni relations, yet she states that "relationship building" is a means of achieving her mission of "providing the financial resources for the university to accomplish its strategic goals." She considers fostering institutional relationships to be the most important part of her job as vice president of development. As we will see in more detail later, her mission filter affects her choice of organizational focus and affects her approach to developing large-gift strategies.

Mission Modification: In Summary

Examining the VPs' modifications to a normative advancement mission statement provides insights into the participant's leadership theory and his or her placement within the management-leadership lens. We begin to see the kaleidoscope effect of the four cornerstones within the Advancement Constellation.

Being clear about mission enables participants like Alex to act quickly to build a bridge or others like Terry to challenge a wealthy donor. As you will see in chapter 2, being clear about mission enables Jo to coalesce her organization.

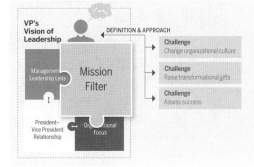

This close scrutiny of the mission modifications lays the foundation for greater understanding of how each of the 10 VPs envisions advancement leadership. This section raises a number of questions for you to consider:

- How is your approach to challenges affected by the filter you apply to the "mission" of raising money?
- Which filter affects your management/leadership style the most: institutional priorities; raising the maximum money; the long-term focus of the institution; or building relationships?
- Is your filter as important as the mission itself? How might your filter affect other parts of your job?

WHAT MAKES YOUR RELATIONSHIP TO YOUR BOSS SO COMPLICATED?

Are university presidents perceived as leaders, fundraisers, icons, or bosses? Or are they seen as all of these?

Lee describes the president as a visionary. Pat talks about the president being a critical actor in the VP's mission to raise money for the priorities of the university. All the vice presidents say the president is a colleague. Recognizing whether that colleague relationship is described as that of boss or team member helps elucidate the VP's position within the management-leadership lens.

Several researchers have studied institutional leadership from the university president's perspective (Bensimon 1990; Bongila 2003; Bornstein 2008; Cohen, March, and Carnegie Commission 1986; Duderstadt 2007; Haden 2000; Madsen 2004; McLaughlin 1996, 2004; McLaughlin and Riesman 1990; Michael, Schwartz, and Balraj 2001). Some of these scholars discuss the importance of the relationship of the institution's president and advancement vice president—from the perspective of the president. This section examines the role of the president from the perspective of the vice president. We learn more about each participant's leadership vision, management-leadership lens, and mission filter. In all of their stories, we learn the ways the multifaceted president–vice president relationship is critical to the advancement leader.

President as Leader

Some presidents are admired because they set high standards, because they envision the university's bright future, because they captivate constituents, and because they model the behavior that they ask of others. Such statements of admiration, made by VPs when talking about a university president, are evidence that the VPs view the president as an example of a good leader, even if they do not make that statement explicitly. As noted previously in the discussion of the leadership lens, many of the participants describe these qualities as critical components of leadership. Setting high standards is akin to being committed to a task, to a plan, to a set of goals, or to accomplishments of some sort. Several participants talk about a president walking into a room and captivating an audience. Others talk about the way members of the university community respond to the dissemination of the president's strategic vision. Other participants talk about feeling grateful for the opportunity to work with a president who embodies those values and behaviors that form the core of the university mission.

Lee admires the "simple elegance" of his president's vision—one of the keys to being a good leader, from his perspective. We see in his choice of words—"she captured the essence of what the university can be"—how he sees her inspiring and thinking of the future. He underscores the president's commitment to her vision and her values by saying that "she lives by those principles." We get a deeper understanding of Lee's management-leadership lens when we look closely at the way Lee talks about the institution president and consider his leadership theory. In this case, Lee's version of a leader is someone who articulates clear values and then drives business with these clear values.

In some cases, the participant explicitly references the president as a model leader and then clarifies his or her thinking by offering an illustration or a story. Jo, for example, states that her president is a real visionary who backs up his visions with actions. She specifically notes he is not a manager.

> But I do think there are different kinds of leadership. So [her president], for example, has the vision and then hires people like [another vice president] and me who work for him and are real self-starters and that he doesn't have to micromanage.

Jo implies that good managers take initiative and get tasks done. In this description and in this situation, she portrays herself as a manager in relationship to her visionary president.

At another point, Jo offers an example of a different university leader who is a good manager as well as a good leader. When we examine what, according to Jo, makes him a good manager/good leader and contrast her statements about the new dean with her statements about the university president, we get a more complete portrait of her leadership theory. In this particular story, she says the new dean is ready to make tough financial decisions in a direct manner, because the situation calls for such toughness and directness. Offering two contrasting examples of leaders reinforces her statement that "there are a lot of different ways that people lead."

Later in our interview, Jo wonders aloud whether this new dean will be able to be visionary (like her institution's president) when the tough financial decisions are behind him. This helps us see what she means by leadership being somewhat situational: When the situation changes, will the new dean have the ability to apply other notions of leadership? As we examine how Jo talks about leadership and her president in the two examples she provides, we gain a deeper understanding of Jo's leadership theory. In addition, Jo's statements show that she looks out of the management-leadership lens according to the demands of the situation. In this section we see, through her comments, how she uses the management portion of the lens in relationship to the visionary president; later you will see her looking out of the leadership portion of the lens when the challenge of changing culture calls for it.

Lee and Jo describe their presidents as leaders and in so doing provide rich insights into their own theories of leadership.

President as Fundraiser

Looking at how participants talk about their president vis-à-vis fundraising gives us the opportunity to see them implementing their theories of leadership. For example, Jordan positions his relationship to his president as a fundraising team of two, where it's Jordan's responsibility to develop and balance the president. Through his comments, Jordan enacts his concept that leaders show how things can be done. Since his president is not a seasoned fundraiser, Jordan assumes the responsibility of developing that skill in his president. Looking through Jordan's mission filter, we further understand that Jordan regards the president as a primary member of Jordan's fundraising mission.

> And we've got a new president who started roughly the same time that I did. And so I've got to...
>
> [Interviewer:] Get him inaugurate next week ... Oh my goodness [laughter]
>
> So the learning curve is steep. I have to do this very quickly, make quick judgments, all along not messing up what is a very substantial and successful organization. So I am kind of balancing the two.

Jordan's footing relative to the president is consistent with his footing in his statements about leadership. He uses "I"; he is talking about how he enacts leadership in regard to his president.

In another case, Pat ties the role of her president directly to her primary mission and to her statement that a leader guides the conduct of the organization.

Well, in fact, we look at the involvement of others in the process. How involved was the president in the process? How many calls did the president make? Because the more people that the president is able to touch, the more those relationships are strengthened to the institution.

In this case, she references her president as the symbolic leader of the organization. The president represents the institution, and Pat's clearly stated mission is to foster strong relationships between alumni and donors and the institution, as opposed to creating personal friendships with the advancement vice president. Pat speaks quickly, succinctly, and assuredly. Her manner of speaking reinforces her self-portrait as someone who has a clear sense of values and principles. Her conviction about her mission to encourage authentic life-long institutional relationships enables Pat to lead her staff and her president to facilitate such meaningful connections.

As Pat implies above, the president is seen as a symbol of the institution and has a critical role in the VP's achieving the mission of bringing donors and alumni into a relationship with the institution. Others—such as Sean—share this sense of the president as institutional icon. Sean illustrates his concept of leaders helping people do better than they know how to do by sharing a dramatic story of a non-alumnus who gave a multimillion-dollar gift that no one expected. To clinch the deal, Sean brought the symbol of the institution—the president—to the donor. Sean says, "I brought the president out. He [the donor] wintered in [a wonderful location quite a distance from the university] and I brought the president out to meet with him. And they hit it off." Sean's footing relative to the president demonstrates his sense of agency and his sense that his mission is to use his "fundraising abilities to meet the university's goals."

Several of the participants talk about making fundraising visits with the university president. This frequent mention of such visits implies that most of the VPs see the president as an important resource and aid in achieving the mission of raising money. Another VP describes the precious nature of the president's time in the following way:

> What I tell them all is that they [university presidents] have to trust the chief development officer because that person has a lot to say about how they spend their time, how much time they spend, and who they invest time in/with.

Examining the VPs' talk helps us see a university president as a leader enacting aspects of the participant's leadership theory and as a symbol embodied with power and influence by simply being a university president.

President as Colleague

In this chapter, close inspection of how each participant talks about his or her relationship to the president sheds light on the participant's management-leadership lens. In some cases, the participant describes a boss-employee relationship and other times a team relationship with the president. Some participants focus on multiple ways of relating—depending on the situation.

Terry represents the views of several other VPs when she directly states the importance of the president–vice president relationship:

> I think that the relationship of the vice president of development to the president of the institution is absolutely critical. I think it has so much to do with trust and rapport. You see all kinds of institutions where there is not that rapport between the vice president and president. And it still works. And the money comes in and all of that kind of thing. But I think at its best, there is that kind of understanding and rapport and trust.

Despite the VPs' agreement on the critical nature of the relationship, the rationale each participant supplied to explain why the relationship is critical seems to differ based on the participant leadership theory and mission filter.

For example, according to Terry's vision of leadership, integrity is of paramount importance, and her mission is to build "community dedicated to the goals of the institution." Building community, in Terry's words, relies on trust and rapport as the foundation of relationships. *Community* does not imply management, but rather implies people relating to each other outside of employee-employer roles. Such a sense of being outside of management-speak aligns with Terry's statement that she is not a student of management or of organizations. Both seem to be key aspects of understanding her placement relative to the management-leadership lens; it seems that she situates herself in community and not in such a lens.

Like Jo, Terry notes that there are multiple ways to achieve the mission of the VP, and she is focused on achieving the "best" kind of president–vice president relationship. This talk supports Terry's description of the single most important aspect of a talented fundraiser and a talented manager: the ability to listen. While in her comments she does not explicitly state that she "listens" to the president, we can infer from how carefully Terry listened during the interview, as well as how Terry talks about her relationship to the president, that Terry does listen.

Sandy, also, emphasizes trust as a critical element of her relationship to her president. In addition to noting the importance of the relationship to the president, Sandy's comments here demonstrate her leadership theory:

> Why that has to be a very close relationship. Close in a sense that there has to be complete trust on his [the president's] part in me and on my part in him. But you know it has to come from me. And one of competence. He needs to have the feeling that my advice is good advice. He needs to feel that I have the institution's priorities and best interest in mind in everything that I am doing. That I have the institutional perspective in mind—not a narrow, you know, interest in mind. And he needs to know that he can absolutely rely on me. By that I mean in anything he needs, in anything he wants, and rely on me in giving him and nudging him and moving the agenda along.

While trust is important, she says that the president's trust originates in Sandy's actions. Through this description, Sandy positions herself in a service role and we gain a better understanding of her leadership theory: "the best VPs are those who see themselves in a service role." Additionally, the way in which she talks of her president positions her in the manager portion of the management-leadership lens, because she says that good managers "take responsibility and accountability to make sure that things go all right." By looking through Sandy's lens at her relationship to her president, we gain a better understanding of Sandy's leadership theory and her focus on service.

All of the participants' talk underscores the importance of the president–vice president relationship. In the two examples above, trust is critical. Another participant emphasizes confidence when talking about the lack of trust that unpredictable behavior fosters. Most participants consider credibility to be an essential component of the president–vice president relationship; some VPs talk about support or lack of support as important to the president–vice president relationship. In one case, the lack of backing was described as "second guessing" the participant and was perceived to make the partici- pant's goals more difficult to achieve. Often, inspecting the aspects of the president–vice president relationship that each participant emphasizes enables us to see the participant enacting his or her leadership theory.

Boss-Employee Relationship

To understand the ways that the VP positions him- or herself in relation- ship to the president, we need to examine more closely their talk about the relationship. Some of these participants describe presidents as accomplished academicians who are not responsible for functional responsibilities attributed to managers. In fact, as previously mentioned, some participants clearly state that the president is not a manager and is not responsible for managing the VP. While each participant acknowledges reporting to the president, a careful examination of how the VP positions him- or herself in the boss-employee relationship helps clarify the VP's focal point within the management-leadership lens. This may provide no contradiction for the participant, or it may serve as a point of tension—depending upon the degree of overlap of management with leadership in the eyes of the participant.

Gene, for example, describes his president as an eminent scholar who in conjunction with the trustees establishes the direction for the university. Gene does not talk about participating in creating that vision; rather, he talks about implementing the vision—a characteristic that he attributes to managers. He considers himself the "lead plumber" and not someone top donors want to see; the president is the person donors want to see. Gene describes the president and one of her "second lieutenants" managing the relationship with the trustees. Gene's description of his relationship to the president, his leadership theory, and his mission reveals evidence of a potential conflict. According to Gene's theory, leaders have vision and strategy to move an organization forward, yet he does not position himself as participating in the grander vision of the university; his focus is on the development office of the university. He says that his president believes the university should be optimized, but Gene's comments reflect his focus on optimizing the development office. In his relationship to the president, he is positioning himself as an expert manager who is implementing a vision he attributes to his president—that is, to modernize. In relationship to potential donors he is an expert "plumber"—not someone who is providing vision. In both of these remarks, Gene seems to be oriented more toward the management side of the management-leadership lens.

By applying the mission filter, the potential tension between management and leadership becomes more evident. Gene says that he is passionate about the mission of higher education, yet he does not participate in establishing the broader university mission. Is Gene simply enacting a boss-employee relationship, or is this evidence of a tension in Gene's leadership theory? Exploring the case of one characterization of the boss-employee relationship exemplifies one dimension of the intricate relationship and of the additional leadership questions close examination stimulates.

Team Relationship

Several VPs talk about being at the "president's table" as a metaphor for a place where decisions get made. This metaphor helps situate the participant as a member of a team led by the owner of the table—the president. A close look at what Alex says about the senior team of his university demonstrates his leadership theory and hints at how his management-leadership lens works relative to developing large gift strategy:

> The vice president should be—I think—intimately involved in the strategic planning of a solicitation. First of all, we have more access to the breadth of the university than anyone else in our organization. We sit around the president's table. We sit around the president's senior staff table.

This comment shows Alex as a member of a team making decisions about the direction or strategy of his institution. The way he constructs this talk portrays him as having a clear idea of what should be done (involve the vice president in strategic planning) and why it should be done (vice president has access to a breadth of information). Alex's talk shows him enacting a "commitment to the individuals and the institution"—a key element of his definition of leadership. In addition to illuminating Alex's previous comments about leadership, his talk about the president's table gives us an appreciation for the way that his mission filter works. Alex says that the mission of his office is to serve as a link between "individuals and the ideas that live at [his university]." His talk shows him striving to ensure that the plan for creating the link is fully grounded in the best information available about the university.

The same participant may choose to view the president–vice president relationship through different parts of the management-leadership lens, depending on the situation. For example, Alex's comments situate him at times as someone who takes direction from the president and builds the president's vision. He says, "The priorities are by and large generated by the president and handed down to the vice president of development." In this case, he is situating himself as a person responsible for building the bridge as opposed to envisioning the bridge. This demonstrates that sometimes Alex views his relationship to the president from a team member stance and sometimes from a manager's perspective.

Critical and Complex President–Vice President Relationship: In Summary

To more fully grasp the participant's decision-making process relative to significant challenges, we need to consider the participant's placement in the management-leadership lens, the participant's mission filter, and how the participant talks about the president. The critical and complicated president–vice president relationship may provide the participant a leadership model, may serve as an integral figure in the participant's advancement plan, and/ or may portray the president as the "boss."

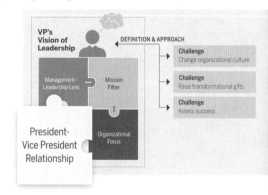

Several participants describe the president in multiple lights, while others rarely reference the president. Yet even a lack of reference to the institution's president sheds light on the participant's perspective on leadership. In higher education, this important relationship is mirrored in the dean–development director relationship; in other nonprofits, this complicated relationship may be evident in the CEO–board president relationship.

Examining the varied ways VPs navigate their relationships to their presidents helps us appreciate the complexity of leading an advancement organization and signals the importance of considering one's own vision of leadership.

WHO ARE YOU LEADING?
WHAT IS YOUR ORGANIZATIONAL FOCUS?

Almost all the vice presidents talk about the breadth of the VP role. Some describe the 24/7 nature of the job; others say the scale of the job is "huge." In an effort to understand the scope of the job, I asked the VPs these questions:

- How do you talk to the various members of your audience?
- Who are the members of your audience?

Understanding how participants answer these questions helps us grasp the VPs' organizational focus, which is another critical aspect of how participants construct leadership in the world of philanthropy in higher education.

Since each VP has a limited amount of time to interact with members of his or her defined audience, decisions about audience boundaries and directing participant energy within those boundaries reveal the participant's management of his or her accountability to the audience members. None of the 10 VPs discussed the choice of focus as a problem. I have chosen to make it problematic to help reveal assumptions about advancement leadership embedded in word choice, constituent maps, prioritization of constituents, and accountability to constituent groups. Existing research on institutional theory, organizational development, and governance underscores the complex setting of the participants' stories of defining and managing constituents.[3] Organizational focus—the final building block in the Advancement Constellation—completes the foundation for each VP's leadership vision, adds more texture to the advancement landscape, and sets the stage for clarifying vantage point.

Organization, Stakeholder, or Constituent?

Consider the different terms used to discuss the concept of the body of people who comprise the VP's audience and the subtle difference those word choices convey. For some, the word *organization* means the participant's staff. For others it refers to the administrative body of the institution, while others consider anyone who is on campus to be the "organization," and still others seem to equate *organization* with constituency.

For example, Jordan uses the term *organization* to refer to his staff, the president, and the provost until I broaden the term and align it with *constituency*. At that point in our conversation, Jordan accepts the alignment by responding with a discussion of volunteers and how he will coach his staff to interact with volunteers. Looking at how Jordan describes talented staff in the ranks of the organization demonstrates Jordan's positioning himself as leading his staff. When he does so, Jordan's focus is his staff. Thus we see Jordan using *organization* in different ways, and each use adds granularity to his vision of leadership.

Some participants respond to questions about stakeholders with answers about constituents, and others incorporate the use of the word *stakeholder* into the discussion. None of the participants uses the word *stakeholder* in our discussions without my first using the word, whereas several of them use the word *constituency* prior to my introducing it. This suggests that some of the participants may be more comfortable talking about their audience as constituents rather than stakeholders. According to the American Heritage College Dictionary (2004), *constituent* is defined as serving as part of a whole or empowered to elect; *stakeholder* is one who is entrusted with the money of bettors or one that has an interest in an enterprise.

Chris does not use the word *constituent* during any of her interviews. Her first use of the word *organization* references her staff, and she continues to use it in that way consistently throughout her talk. In response to my question about her audiences and my suggestion of the term *stakeholders,* she responds as follows:

> Stakeholders. Right. Right. The ... certainly ... the corporation is one audience. ... [Another audience is] our senior operating team—operating managers.

When we consider Chris's use of the term *organization,* her response above, and her leadership theory, we see Chris focuses her talk of leadership on her staff and her institution's executive governing body. Thus a close examination of her use of the word *organization* helps clarify her choice of organizational focus as well as her vision of leadership. Both clarifications will be useful in understanding how she approaches key challenges.

In contrast, Jo uses *organization* broadly, referring to the spectrum of possible constituents. She first uses the term in reference to alumni of the institution and then later in reference to the development staff. Jo's confident and rapid response to the question of audience indicates her defining the broad organization as her general audience. Her specific text below shows her sense of priority within the general audience.

> Q: When you were describing "It's in the eye of the beholder," who do you consider to be your key "beholders"—or stakeholders might even be a word.

> First the president and trustees because those are the people to whom I'm directly accountable and to whom I directly report. And then I would say next on that would be the deans and the faculty. The alumni—I don't think about my relationship in terms of—kind of from a fundraising perspective—being accountable to the alumni, but I think on an alumni relations basis they would certainly be the number one stakeholders. And then students might be the second group—looking from an alumni relations perspective at the kind of culture that we're trying to get them to think about while they're here as students. So in that case it is sort of different between development and alumni relations.

As with Jordan and Chris, Jo's choice of words and description of her audience provide insights into her choice of focus—the broad spectrum—and into her concept that leadership is somewhat situational.

The subtle choice to use or not to use the more business-like term *stakeholder* helps us understand organizational focus. Several of the VPs preferred to use *constituency* rather than *stakeholder* when talking about their organization. As you can see in Jo's comments above, many vice presidents reference being accountable to constituents and look for ways to include key constituents in their decision-making process. The sense of accountability and desire for input on key decisions seems akin to what one would expect to find among people who have been elected to their posts, but advancement vice presidents are *not* elected. Several participants describe organizational concerns often associated with building political bases, such as acknowledging multiple audiences and attention to relationships.[4]

Jo's talk demonstrates all three aspects of this close alignment of constituency and organization: the metaphor of the "eye of the beholder" suggests many eyes viewing her actions; success is achieved by collaboration, not by decree; and building an organization equates with building relationships. Acknowledging the potential for multiple VP audiences provides insights to job scope and the need to choose—consciously or unconsciously—an organizational focus.

Close examination of word choice helps us understand organizational focus, but it's not enough to answer the question, Who are you leading?

FIGURE 2. A Vice President's Constituents

A VP's vision of leadership and institutional environment dynamically interacts with his or her definition and approach to significant challenges

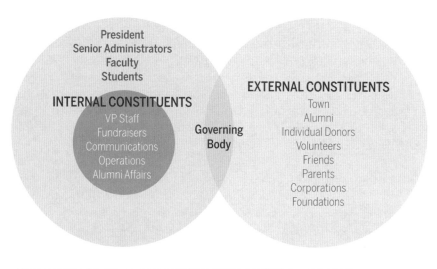

BROAD SPECTRUM (ALL CONSTITUENTS)

President
Senior Administrators
Faculty
Students

INTERNAL CONSTITUENTS
VP Staff
Fundraisers
Communications
Operations
Alumni Affairs

**Governing
Body**

EXTERNAL CONSTITUENTS
Town
Alumni
Individual Donors
Volunteers
Friends
Parents
Corporations
Foundations

Composite Constituent Diagram

Based on the 10 participants' discussion of constituents, figure 2 presents a composite perspective of a VP's environment. All the potential audiences are itemized and grouped using bold titles and shading.

Each of the VPs mentioned a different mix of the groups listed in the figure, varying in focus and comprehensiveness. This composite map illuminates the complex environment in which the VP functions.

Prioritization of Constituents Reveals Focus

Further close examination of the VPs' discussion of audience suggests the VP chooses a focus within the composite map. The VPs tended to exhibit focus on one of the three main areas shown in figure 2: broad spectrum, internal constituents, or VP staff. For example, Lee says he must report his success and failures to all his constituencies, who he describes as all groups shown in the figure. A key aspect of his responsibility to his constituency includes reporting on financial matters to the deans and center directors who, in his view, fund his operation. Part of the road map he sees as critical to leadership is accounting for the financial variables both in terms of money raised and in terms of money spent. At one point Lee says:

> And one of the first things that I did was open up the budgets and laid them out in front of people—did a complete review. And the deans had never seen that before. So this is where money is being spent and this is where I think that we need to go. And work with them in terms of a formula. You can usually trace most issues back to money. So that was the one that I went after first.

In this comment, Lee emphasizes the deans as a key audience and illustrates his focus on budget as a road map. Close examination of those constituencies that Lee emphasizes helps us see his focus on the internal senior administrators as key members of his audience. His discussion of the deans aligns with his focus on key values—in this case, transparency. Lee's choice of focus is a clear demonstration of his leadership theory and of the complexity of his particular advancement landscape.

Some participants stated a focus a little more directly than Lee. Sandy says, "Our foremost job is to develop institutional relationships," indicating that her focus is the broad spectrum. This focus ties directly to Sandy's statement of her mission and to her concept of advancement leadership. She says relationship building is a means of providing the institution with the financial resources to accomplish its strategic goals. At another point she says, in response to a question about important relationships within the administration of the university, "If you have good relations with them obviously that greases the wheel, but it's not the same crucial nature as it is to be completely in sync with the academic priorities or the president." The way that Sandy constructs this declaration suggests that understanding the academic priorities of the institution is as important as her relationship to her president. These priorities are critical, and it is around these priorities that Sandy talks about fostering relationships to the institution. Her focus is the broad spectrum because it enables her to achieve her mission, and in so doing she enacts her vision of leadership.

On the other hand, Gene says, "I do—will tell people that I think about every day when I come in—people, processes, and systems," thus indicating his focus on the development staff. At another point he explicitly states, "I spend much more of my time on organizational development, strategy, driving continuous change and improvement, and internally focused aspects of the job, rather than going out to meet with donors." He defines *organization* to be his staff, and most of his talk revolves around his vision of leading his staff to be more "modern" and "professional." Careful examination of how participants vary their attention to different aspects of the composite map helps illuminate a participant's organizational focus.

The Advancement Landscape—A Complex Backdrop

The constituent map in figure 2 illustrates the importance of the individual VP's choice of organizational focus and hints at the complexity of the advancement landscape. The map also implies some governance considerations. Rather than use revealing examples from the participants' individual landscapes to illustrate the complex backdrop, I depend on several scholars' investigation of institutional environment or campus culture to help the reader grasp the importance of context in the advancement leadership decision-making process. A brief look at the inherent complexity of higher education, the differing notions of governance, and the impact of external factors adds color to the backdrop of the Advancement Constellation.

Inherent Complexity

Each of the VPs mentioned some but not all of the constituents in the composite map. This suggests differences between their institutions as well as a difference in their perspectives. Several researchers talk about fundamental differences in peoples' perception of the institution as an entity. For example, Cohen and March (1986) make an eloquent case for colleges and universities being "organized anarchy." They see institutional decision-making processes and outcomes as "loosely coupled." Other researchers like Pusser (2003) advocate for understanding organizational behavior in higher education by understanding the political dynamics of governance and decision making in this context. Although the 10 vice presidents are members of the same university cohort group, their diverse answers to the question, Who are you leading? supports the scholars' descriptions of the modern university as intricate and variable. Each VP emphasizes different aspects of the broad spectrum of constituents and in so doing reveals his or her unique vantage point.

Rather than view the institution as "organized anarchy" or a political arena, I embrace the Bolman and Deal (2003) multi-frame approach. According to Bolman and Deal, there are four common ways of viewing an organization: factory, family, jungle, or theater. Using the Bolman and Deal approach to understand the advancement landscape underscores both the inherent complexity and the importance of the individual leader's vantage point. For example, Jo's vision of success as tied to the "eye of the beholder" is somewhat different from Lee's vision of using transparent budget management to win the support of the deans at his institution. Yet both VPs describe the importance of knowing the particular institution when assessing success. The VPs' different approaches to leadership reveal their different views of the character of higher education in general as well as the differences in their particular institutions. By listening to the VPs' talk of organizational focus and their views of campus culture, we can better appreciate the complex environments in which the VPs make difficult decisions. The challenge of working with, as well as changing, advancement culture is explored in greater depth in chapter 2.

Institutional Governance

Closely related to differing views of the institution as an entity are differing perspectives on institutional governance.[5] In the composite constituent diagram (figure 2), the governing body is central to the diagram. However, not every VP included the university's governing body when talking about constituents. This omission implies the variability of the advancement landscapes within a defined cohort group and lends support to the importance of considering the individual VP's leadership vision within the context of the particular institutional environment. A macro view of the 10 universities represented by the 10 participants supports the scholars' claim to a wide variance in governance structures, ranging from a loose linking of undergraduate and professional schools to a more tightly integrated governance structure. Chapter 2 will explore in more depth the impact of each VP's organizational perspective on his or her approach to key challenges.

McLaughlin, a scholar of university presidents, defines governance as "enlisting others effectively; it involves balancing the interests of multiple constituencies and respecting the process of decision making" (2004, 87). This notion of governance implies an individual who is acting—enlisting, balancing, and respecting.

McLaughlin's definition of governance suggests moving parts as well. As represented in the Advancement Constellation, VPs look at and interact with governance structures, have a perception of the role of conflict in the decision-making process, and intertwine notions of the governance culture into their vantage points. Existing institutional structures and the VP's perspective on the effectiveness of the structures are linked to the

VP's approach to governance. For example, Lee considers that providing transparent budgets to his governing board is critical to his successful leadership. Gene doesn't mention interacting with a governing body.

Just as the individual has a view of the importance of governance structures, the individual VP has a perspective on enlisting and balancing constituent support—McLaughlin's view of governance. In some ways, McLaughlin's concept of governance is similar to Pusser's concept of political modeling, described as the expression of individual preferences. Pusser (2003) goes on to say the consensus-driven culture of higher education masks the effectiveness of political modeling. Both scholars advocate for researchers' examining how external influences and interests interact with institutional governance structures and with institutional administration.

Pusser uses examples from public universities and focuses on the role of state governments to elucidate his notion of interest groups. Perhaps similar dynamics are at play in the universities of the 10 VPs, where alumni play a role similar to the general populace, boards of governors review key administrative practices, and the administrative hierarchy comprises multiple interest groups. In chapter 2, you will hear examples of the different ways in which participants describe "interest groups." Although the VPs in this study did not speak about institutional theory or institutional governance per se, they did talk about the institution as having a knowable character. Without revealing the particulars of each VP's institution, I rely on recent scholarship to help explain how the VP's perspective of institutional governance is a critical component of the dynamic interaction of leadership vision and advancement landscape.

External Factors

Several scholars talk about the importance of considering external factors when approaching significant decisions, or what I refer to as challenges (Chaffee 1987; Clark 1972; Cohen, March, and Carnegie Commission 1986; Heifetz 1994; McLaughlin 2004; Peterson and Mets 1987; Pusser 2003; Williams 2005). Setting a significant decision in the context of time and space implies contrasting the decision with what has previously transpired (McLaughlin 2004; Pettigrew 1977; Pfeffer 1992). Political realities at a local or national or global level, technology, the economy, the media, and social norms all affect the way in which the organization and decision makers interact. Clayton Spencer, vice president for policy at Harvard University, talked about the membrane separating the internal university from the external world. Her description of the interaction of the media, the faculty, the administration, the governing board, and the university president relative to President Summer's remarks about women's innate abilities in math (Spencer 2008) succinctly demonstrates the importance of considering external factors as an integral aspect of the *dynamism* of the Advancement Constellation. In the world of fundraising, these external factors contribute to the level of complexity in the advancement landscape. Chapter 2 offers examples of how external factors intricately interact with the advancement vice president's definition of organizational focus, definition of the challenge, and approach to the challenge.

Understanding Audience and Organizational Focus: In Summary

The choice of words, a constituent mapping, and the prioritization of focus help us better understand the subtle ways participants differ in their views of leadership. In addition to examining particular words as a means of understanding the VPs' definition of organization, carefully listening to the audiences the participant emphasizes provides insights to the VP's choice of focus. We begin to see how who they perceive they are leading affects how they approach challenges.

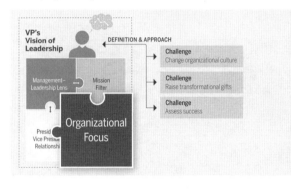

Tying this study's findings to existing research helps define the complexity of the participants' decision-making terrain. Although not explicit, the composite map implies some governance considerations. Given this study's commitment to the privacy of the participants, highlights from existing research help to underscore the importance of institutional environment and external factors to advancement decision making. Chapter 3 delves more deeply into participant perspectives on institutional theory, governance and external factors—although these are not the terms used by the participants.

Through the VPs' candor, the reader gains rare insights into who constitutes the VP's organization and how the VP's organizational focus impacts his or her vision of leadership.

FIGURE 3. Participant Vantage Point

The idea of having a vantage point implies the dimensions of time and place

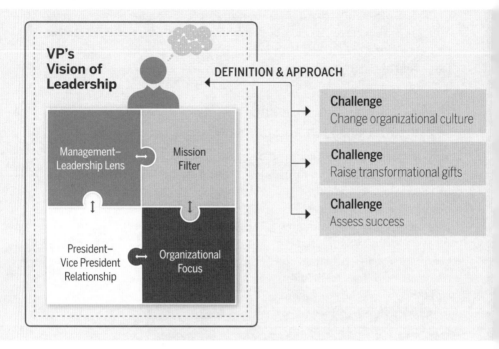

WHAT'S THE DIFFERENCE BETWEEN LEADERSHIP VISION AND VANTAGE POINT?

Jordan and Jo take different approaches to the challenge of changing organizational culture. Their leadership visions are different and their vantage points are different. Applying best practices is *not* a simple "cut and paste" exercise. Lee has a leadership vision *before* he interviews for his new position as VP and he develops his initial vantage point as he executes his entry plan.

The idea of having a vantage point implies the dimensions of time and place. In figure 3, the participant vantage point (encircled, on the left side of the figure) is symbolized by a person contemplating the stars while standing on four dynamically linked cornerstones. The four cornerstones connect to form a participant's leadership theory and to serve as the foundation from which the VP defines and approaches the challenges of the advancement world.

Pat—who sees leadership as having a clearly articulated mission and whose mission is to raise maximum dollars for the institution—chooses to focus on donors and talks about her president primarily in the context of the mission. At a very different institution and at a very different point in that institution's history, Jo—who considers leadership to be situational and who says her mission is to engage constituents as well as raise money—demonstrates a broad focus and talks about relating to her president in multiple lights. Jo talks about being part of the senior team as well as being a manager who supports her visionary president. Their leadership visions are different and their vantage points are different.

Terry says the most important aspect of leadership is integrity, considers her mission to be to build a community geared to raising money for the institution's priorities, and focuses her efforts on a broad definition of community. Terry shares that she made a significant personal decision based on a request from her institution's president: She did what she considered to be best for the institution, demonstrating a trust in her president and a commitment to her community. By taking a holistic view of the participant, we gain a better understanding of the foundation from which each participant enacts his or her definition of leadership when approaching tough challenges.

The porous line separating the VP's vantage point from the institutional environment denotes a bi-directional impact. It suggests movement. Alex's description of his president's inner circle is very different from Gene's description of the decision makers at his institution. Their stories help illuminate their different leadership visions interacting with different institutional governance structures. A follow-up interview with Gene flags the fourth dimension of the dynamic nature of the model. Two years after Gene described his sharp focus on people, processes, and systems, he described a change in his organizational focus. His primary focus moved from staff to include the broader set of constituents. Most of the vice presidents echoed the importance of understanding their thoughts on leadership as "snapshots in time." This fourth dimension of time eludes the flat diagram in figure 3. The notion of vantage point attempts to capture the sense of dynamism suggested by several scholars as critical in the study of leadership.[6] By taking an approach that examines the dynamic interaction of a person with a tough problem, the focus is on the dynamism of the system rather than on the leader's traits or charisma. This dynamism is represented in the Advancement Constellation by the porous line and by several double-pointed arrows. In chapter 1, "Recognizing the Cornerstones of Advancement Leadership," we have established a general framework with moving parts set in the complex advancement landscape.

Benefitting from the Cornerstone Framework: In Summary

The cornerstone framework offers multiple advantages. The importance of fit stands out as paramount to university presidents, vice presidents, nonprofit board presidents, volunteer campaign chairs, and school superintendents: fit of the president and the vice president with each other; fit of the advancement leader with the way the institution is conceived and governed; and fit of the nonprofit leader with the particular needs of the current administration. In this study, only one of the advancement vice presidents was "inherited"; in the nine other cases, the president selected the vice president. Presumably in the recruiting process both president and vice president have an opportunity to consider fit. The search process also offers the prospective advancement director the time to consider his or her leadership vantage point in the light of the environment or current culture of the institution. Search firms regularly experience the patience needed to fit institution, prospective employee, and president.

In some ways, the president–vice president relationship described in this study is similar to the relationship of the volunteer campaign chair or foundation director to the nonprofit's board president. The trust and rapport established between the pair is critical to the success of the campaign. As more and more school districts face budgetary shortfalls and turn to philanthropy as a source of revenue ("New Future" 2008), school superintendents face some of the same questions of fit. For these relative newcomers, the cornerstone framework offers a way to make sense of the new challenge of considering varied constituents, diverse cultures, and alternative funding options.

Being clear with oneself about each cornerstone enables the advancement leader to articulate a holistic leadership vision and to consider other vantage points when approaching challenges. Leadership research indicates the importance of such flexible mental modeling (Bolman and Deal 2003; Heifetz 1994). In this work, Gene demonstrates how such flexibility and creativity benefits the current members of the composite organization and increases his options for success.

Some practitioners may turn to others in search of best practices. The varying vantage points of the 10 participants are helpful exemplars. At the same time, the practitioner is warned of the importance of fit when considering best practices. A leader like Chris benefits from hearing others talk about the importance of "pace" in changing proud cultures yet can't assume Lee's exact entry plan without considering her institution and her president.

Finally, students, researchers, and faculty of advancement in higher education or nonprofit organizations can use this framework to examine an area needing deeper investigation. Is this framework viable for examining advancement leadership in smaller private colleges? Is it applicable to public universities? Is it unique to advancement? How does it apply to nonprofits without a clearly defined constituency? The case examples lend themselves to illustrating the framework and offering insights into real life quandaries.

This first part of *Envisioning Advancement Leadership* has offered a framework for examining participant leadership theories based on an analysis of four common elements across 10 cases. The next part demonstrates how understanding the fundamental components of a VP's leadership vision and vantage point aids in understanding the decisions a participant makes when approaching complex problems in institutional advancement.

NOTES

1. To protect the anonymity of the vice presidents and their institutions the quotes are attributed to a pseudonym; to support the underlying premise of alignment that is critical to the Advancement Constellation, the pseudonyms are used consistently throughout the study.

2. The bracketed numbers refer to lines from the interview as captured in the transcriptions.

3. While the intertwining and application of these ideas to advancement leadership is mine, deeper treatment of each concept can be found in existing research on political processes (Bolman and Deal 2003; Dill and Fullagar 1987; Bennis and Nanus 2003; Heifetz 1994; McLaughlin 1996; McLaughlin 2004; Pfeffer 1992; Burns 1979; French and Raven 1986; Rogers and Roethlisberger 1991; Julius, Baldridge, and Pfeffer 1999; Pettigrew, 1977; Kotter 1996; Tierney and Lechuga 2004; Tucker 1995).

I rely on leadership research describing the variability and importance of individual perspective (Bolman and Deal 2003; Dill and Fullagar 1987) to support my close examination of the VPs' choice of words.

I introduce constituent mapping (Bolman and Deal 2003; Heifetz 1994; Kotter 1996; Keohane 1985; Pusser 2003) to extend the discussion of variability and to introduce the need for difficult choices.

Finally, I situate the work of advancement in the complex university organization or environment described by several scholars (Peterson and Mets 1987; Pusser 2003; Chaffee 1987).

While grounding my analysis in existing research, I believe there is much more to learn by investigating the role of rhetoric and the relevance of political processes to advancement leadership.

4. Several researchers have explored the connection between political power and leadership (Bennis and Nanus 2003; Burns 2006; Pfeffer 2010), but fewer have set their research in the context of higher education (Pusser and Doane 2001). There is a great open opportunity to determine what strong research in the world of business and politics can be transferred successfully to the advancement landscape.

5. Three slightly different scholarly perspectives of governance in higher education further illuminate the complex and variable advancement backdrop:

1. governance structures have an inherent tension (Birnbaum 2004),

2. universities emphasize consensus-driven decision making (Pusser 2003), and

3. individual actions play a key role (McLaughlin 2004).

The notion of inherent tension in institutional governance sheds light on the idea of moving parts in the Advancement Constellation. Some scholars—such as Pusser (2003)—see the resolution of institutional conflict resulting in consensus-driven decision making and deem this a form of collegial dysfunction.

Pfeffer, another organizational theorist, links a common ambivalence for using power to lessons learned in school where the focus is on individual effort and definitive answers (Pfeffer 1992). Both Pusser and Pfeffer agree that power and conflict are integral to decision making and to the governance culture of an institution. These three perspectives add color and are not mutually exclusive.

6. Several scholars argue for using a multifaceted approach to studying the dynamics of leadership. For example, Wheatley (2006) contends a holistic approach provides a deeper understanding.

In his book *Leadership Without Easy Answers*, Heifetz (1994) provides three reasons for using his interactive approach to examining leadership:

• a belief that many problems are embedded in complicated and interactive systems,

• a bias that people's actions result from adapting to circumstances, and

• a view of leadership as service

In order to demonstrate people adapting to circumstances, Heifetz separates challenges into different levels of complexity and argues that the most difficult problems—those without easy answers—benefit from taking a holistic view of the problem.

CHAPTER 2

FITTING
VANTAGE POINT WITH CHALLENGE

Grouping the many concerns voiced by the advancement vice presidents into three key challenges provides valuable insights into the relationship of leadership perspective and decision making. Each challenge is multi-dimensional and does not appear to have an easy answer. As Ron Heifetz (1994) would say, such challenges require flexible and creative decision making. If one takes a wide-angle view of each of these challenges, the participants' combined description of the inherent issues illustrates the complex environments in which these participants operate. Once again, to protect the privacy and well-being of each participant, chapter 2 does not examine in-depth all the intricacies of the particular environments. For example, institutional constraints such as size, location, endowment, economic climate, governance structure, and president's perspective are not explored. However, by listening closely to the participants' stories, we gain an understanding of the dynamic interaction of their vantage point and the common challenges they face within a particular snapshot in time. Throughout chapter 2, we see how, in Max DePree's words, "The visible signs of artful leadership are expressed, ultimately, in its practice" (1989, 148).

At a high level, the first challenge presented here ("Preserving or Changing Organizational Culture") provides a collective view of some of the thorny aspects of assessing organizational culture. When examined as individual stories, the participants' varying approaches to the culture challenge reflect each leader's manner of intertwining the four leadership cornerstones: perspective on management-leadership, mission filter, president–vice president relationship, and choice of focus. Through an examination of the interaction of vantage point and challenge, the reader gains a better understanding of the importance of fit.

Challenge 2, "Developing Large Gift Strategies," explores the participants' difficulty in defining the challenge. The multifaceted nature of this challenge reveals deeper understanding of their varying leadership theories and suggests critical questions to ask regarding large gift strategies.

The final challenge, "Assessing Success," offers a composite description of the complications in evaluating advancement success and illustrates two different approaches to this common challenge. Again, the dynamic interaction of the participant leadership theory, environment, and the particular challenge recommends the importance of fit.

Using the Advancement Constellation model as a road map for examining each challenge provides the reader with a holistic view of advancement leadership. No approach is touted as "best practice." Instead, the use of the Advancement Constellation encourages the reader to understand the leader's decisions in relationship to the challenge's moving parts.

Challenge 1

PRESERVING OR CHANGING ORGANIZATIONAL CULTURE

During their interviews, all of the participants referenced at least some aspect of culture and many spoke at some length about the importance or role or challenge of culture. Jordan's statement represents comments by several participants:

> Understanding the culture is critical I think. Every culture is slightly differ-
> ent. University X certainly had a very unique culture to it. Understanding
> how each college was kind of a tub on its own bottom and how each
> dean was viewed almost as a president of their own little college and had
> tremendous influence and power. ... [It] was a different model than I had
> seen, frankly, before at public institutions.

Like Jordan, several participants refer to the university as an entity with a personality or culture. At times the whole university is painted with a broad brushstroke—entrepreneurial or collegial, for example. Some participants talk about the strength of their particular institution's culture and about how the culture has an impact on strategies, interactions, or even the ability to achieve success. Some talk about being hired to change the culture of the office or the culture of the senior staff or the culture of the interaction with alumni. Others talk about needing to understand the culture in order to preserve its virtues. In all cases, Jordan's observation rings true: Understanding culture is critical.

For purposes of this study, the term *culture* refers to a group's most significant shared values. There are many more aspects of culture that could and have been examined in higher education, in philanthropy, and in leadership. However, by constraining my attention to valued behaviors, the participants' descriptions and approaches are more crisply portrayed.

What Makes Changing or Preserving Culture a Challenge?

Participants talk about several difficult aspects of changing what a group values or the way decisions are made in the group. In most cases the partici-pants discuss valuing a particular behavior such as volunteer engagement. For example, Jordan says, "Well, we have a combination of a very, very active volunteer network and regional programs that engage volunteerism at a very, very high level." Jordan describes needing to understand how that aspect of the volunteer culture works before he changes it. Articulating significant aspects of culture and then taking the time to understand the current culture make change difficult.

In addition to the time it takes to learn the culture, the weight of tradition is another factor most participants talk about that makes change a slow and arduous process. They say that habit causes people to continue to search for VPs who are also alumni of the university or to expel people who have not grown up in the culture. Sometimes the participants articulate the values they want to engender in their organization. For example, Lee explicitly says he values collegiality, collaboration, and transparency. Other participants are not as explicit; in these cases, I will demonstrate through an examination of word choice, focal point, and use of metaphors the implied behaviors they value.

Most participants talk about the pressure of time causing them to press for rapid change—sometimes more rapidly than their constituents can manage. They describe searching for incentives to encourage speedy adjustments to behavior. Many speak about the need to identify clear, measurable indicators of change. Yet some warn of the dangers of trying to measure certain valued behaviors. Others talk about the need to balance—to preserve the good aspects of present culture while inviting innovative solutions to perplexing problems.

For several the scale of change presents the greatest obstacle. They talk about global alumni networks or each of many schools having a different set of norms. A few speak about the strenuousness of changing people's thinking as a first step to changing people's behavior. Some speak eloquently about the interdependencies of culture with funding models, presidential leadership, or governance structures. Some VPs attribute cultural characteristics to the nature of higher education or to the nature of philanthropy. They say the conviction of the faculty or the solo nature of a professor's work translates to a culture that does not reward or value collaboration.

I claim that the different approaches the participants describe for bringing about desired behaviors flashes their leadership theories into stark relief. The following vignettes demonstrate the varying approaches to changing and preserving culture.

Jordan Changes Volunteer Culture and Sean Preserves

Participants talk about a volunteer's relationship to the institution or to the advancement staff. They discuss the quality and level of the volunteer relationship, and they share ways to make the relationship a positive experience that is meaningful to the volunteer. Some VPs discuss the desired role of a volunteer or the historic role of the volunteer. Some VPs track the many ways in which individual constituents volunteer and value most those volunteers deemed to be leaders; other VPs suggest that such individual tracking of the aspects of the volunteer relationship jeopardizes developing good relations. Often when referencing volunteers as leaders, a VP is implying that the volunteer is "leading" the giving effort for some set of donors; but sometimes the VP means that a volunteer is leading by performing some governance role. The following close examination of the varying ways Jordan and Sean talk about engaging volunteers demonstrates how each participant's leadership theory dynamically interacts with the VP's complex environment and the challenge of changing culture.

Being strategic is a key element of Jordan's leadership theory and is reflected in his assessment of potential changes he would like to make to his institution's volunteer network. Jordan says he is concerned about assessing the "boundary of volunteer involvement" and wants to find ways to identify an appropriate boundary while encouraging volunteers to take ownership. As a relatively new member of the university, he expresses concern about understanding the culture before making changes and implementing his vision. He wants to preserve what works and introduce changes that work too. Thus he talks about pacing and balancing change. He goes on to say, "So I will encourage that, with some focus and some direction that has probably not been seen quite at the level that I want [here]." This statement mirrors Jordan's theory that a leader needs to be positive and to show people how things are done. Implied in Jordan's approach to changing the ways volunteers are engaged is the way that his staff will interact with volunteers, thus echoing Jordan's focus on his staff to provide increased direction to volunteers.

Sean's concept of leadership is "inspiring people to do better than they know how to do," and his approach to engaging volunteers demonstrates his leadership theory. He talks about having a "pretty heavy—pretty active volunteer list for this campaign." Changing from the use of the word *heavy* to the use of *active* demonstrates Sean's sense that he is stretching himself as well as the volunteers to do more than he or they might think possible.

He goes on to quantify the extent to which this volunteer culture is more expansive than any with which he has worked previously. Here's how he describes his objective:

> It's still staff driven in many ways, but we're really trying in earnest to use our volunteers—to broaden our reach, to broaden our solicitation, and to heighten awareness about the campaign.

In Sean's approach to volunteers, we see him enacting his mission to use his fundraising abilities to meet the institution's goals. While Jordan talks about potentially defining the boundary more tightly, Sean talks about expanding the boundary—evidence of two different approaches to changing the volunteer culture and each indicative of the VP leadership theory.

Jo Transforms Institutional Attitude

Jo summarizes her goal of changing culture as "transforming our attitude—our institutional attitudes about alumni relations as well as development." With these words she succinctly identifies a difficult challenge and conveys her focus on the broad spectrum of the institutional constituency. *Transforming* suggests a significant alteration rather than minor modifications. And true to her concept of teamwork, Jo indicates through the use of "our" that she is an active participant in addressing this challenge. Jo is not trying to transform behavior; instead, she wants to transform the underlying attitudes across the institution about two significant ways that the alumni interact with the institution. Jo's concise description of her goal demonstrates her tackling a challenge that encompasses several of the more thorny aspects described by her colleagues. Examining her approach brings to light her choice of focus, her relationship to her president, her mission filter, and the management-leadership lens.

The breadth of the challenge is "institutional," implying that all constituents will be touched. She talks about undertaking the process of changing the alumni's perspective on the culture by "trying to get them to think about it while they're here as students." She talks about forming staff-alumni or staff-volunteer partnerships, and she describes hiring a consulting firm to survey many, many alumni. Her organizational focus is broad, and this scope is reflected in her definition of the challenge.

Jo says leadership entails an ability to stay focused on the big picture and to take advantage of opportunities. Her talk demonstrates the way she has enacted both of these aspects of leadership. She says, "Everything we've been doing in the last four years has been—starting with Bob's[1] inaugural address—has been saying to alumni, 'We want to change the way the university interacts with and connects with alumni and the way alumni connect with each other.'" All actions are focused on the goal of transforming institutional attitudes. She describes her alumni as having a "real openness on their part to hear a different story." Jo sees an opportunity with the governing body—the trustees—to listen to a different path and talks about how she is leveraging the trustees' openness to create a new alumni association headed by one of the trustees. It's part of Jo's leadership theory to seize opportunities and recognize the situational aspects of leading.

Jo describes her president's support as another positive aspect of the situation. She says, "Bob already understood the importance of investing in development and that you can't—from the work we've done together at [a previous university]—and that you can't divorce—you really don't want to divorce development and alumni relations." This talk demonstrates Jo's concept of her president as an integral part of her mission's success. Her simple reference to a previous institution where she and Bob worked underlines the importance of trust and support that comes from developing a strong working relationship. In the way that she talks about her president, Jo implies that she approaches each member of her constituency looking for support. She says "Bob already understood," so she did not have to convince him or change his thinking; he already understood. From other aspects of Jo's talk about her president, we know she considers him to be inspiring and visionary. Through close examination of Jo's word choice, we see the importance of this cornerstone to Jo and to her approach to the mammoth challenge of changing institutional attitudes.

Describing Bob's expression of support as "investing" hints at the interdependencies Jo describes. She talks about not having enough money to invest in alumni programs because of a previous focus on raising money for immediate needs. She talks about certain fundraising programs being "bankrupt" because of a lack of regard for the long term. Jo says she is the vice president of both alumni relations and development. By drawing attention to the structure of her responsibility set and the structure of her staff organization, Jo demonstrates alignment of her definition of the culture challenge with her mission of raising money and friends for the long term. She points to the structure of the finances as well as the structure of the staff as two critical components to her achieving her goal of transforming culture.

Jo's talk of transforming staff attitudes shows aspects of how she exercises her management-leadership lens. Similar to Lee's clarity of values, Jo articulates several core values: respect, civility, responsibility, accountability, teamwork, collaboration, and trustworthiness. She describes the challenge being much more difficult than she expected and taking much longer than she expected. Jo tells a story of creating a poster with the core values listed so each member of the staff could show their commitment to the values by signing it. Jo says she signed first as a symbolic gesture. Her story shows how she makes things happen and shows her willingness to be, in her words, "kind of hokey" to prove her commitment to the values she said were important. Close examination of her story shows Jo finding ways to "inspire people to kind of lift up"—another key aspect of her leadership theory.

According to Jo's theory of leadership, you have to "earn respect, build relationships, and find opportunities." In each of the ways she approaches her goal of transforming institutional attitudes, we see Jo fostering relationships. In the many story fragments she shares, her active balancing of management and leadership shines through. She says:

> Whether it's the difference between staff-driven and volunteer-driven organizations, and you're looking for that partnership or the sense about management and leadership kind of stuff, and I find that that's the hardest to describe—because it's easier to describe extremes and it's the hardest to maintain because it almost is that feeling that [on] any day [there are] forces pushing you in both directions and it's much easier to just go to one extreme.

The dynamic interaction of personal leadership theory, institutional environment, and challenge is evident by examining Jo's description of changing institutional attitudes.

Lee Changes University Senior Staff Culture

Lee says:

> Creating cultures can take a long time. The key piece then is to look at what are the existing barriers to that. When you hire people with the expectation and from the very top the leadership is such that you expect that to happen—and the constituencies to which you serve, whether they are the students or the faculty, expect that to occur, then I think you can have an impact. And I think that's in part—if you go back 20 or 25 years—then

misery loves company, all the deans are sitting in the same boat, they're all suffering under RCM and so that means that they carry all of the deferred maintenance, all the maintenance in construction of projects, and they have to hit their bottom line so they have to be able to finance that. So they're all in it together, but then they look at opportunities at how we can leverage. So there are incentives to be entrepreneurial.

Like his colleagues, Lee advocates understanding the culture of an institution as a first step in the process of determining potential changes to established norms. In addition to talking about identifying existing barriers, he talks about seeking the perspective of current and former constituents such as trustees, faculty, and staff. He sees the entrepreneurial culture of the university growing out of the interdependencies of the university financial structure that provide incentives to the deans to treat their units as independent business units and his own staff members who offer services to the deans in exchange for a budget transfer from the dean's budget to Lee's budget. He recognizes that the entrepreneurial nature of his university also creates a propensity to "hold everything close." True to his leadership theory, Lee espouses three core values as critical to his approach to changing the way business is conducted across the administrative units of the university: collegiality, collaboration, and transparency. Lee says there is a high level of accountability demanded in the current advancement culture, and in his assessment his university's deans will respond to a transparent discussion of Lee's budget. He talks about the importance of an organization encouraging matrix management. He says, "I think that matrix creates a fabric by which you can build a culture." Like his president, Lee advocates clear values and then enacts those values.

Lee's approach to preserving the entrepreneurial culture and advocating for collaboration in the senior administration demonstrates the four cornerstones of Lee's leadership theory: his choice to *focus* on the deans and their budgets; his concept of a *leader* enacting core values; his definition of his *mission* being to move the philanthropic program at the university to a higher level; and his concept of supporting the key values of his *president*. By balancing the good aspects of the culture with the changes he values, Lee's talk shows him accounting for the large variables in his road map to success.

As was evident in Lee's approach, Chris's experience changing senior staff culture provides several insights about her leadership theory. She says, "I totally under-appreciated the strength of the culture and the difficulty of making changes. I think that had I to do it over again I think that I would move more slowly." Chris says she was hired to move things at a faster pace, to be aggressive, and to be innovative. She says she was unable to achieve a faster pace because her speed was out of sync with the culture of her senior staff. She describes the decision-making process at the university as succumbing to the "weight of tradition." She says in other venues the decision-making process is participatory, "but then the decision is made and you just sort of go with it." Chris's approach to changing the culture of the senior advancement staff evidences a conflict between her mission, her vision of management-leadership, and her approach to the culture challenge. She resolves this conflict by saying if she had it to do over again, she would treat the senior staff more as constituents whose support she needed to garner and pace her introduction of change accordingly. In saying this, Chris shows that she is reflecting on how to dynamically fit her leadership theory to the challenge and the environment.

Gene and Terry Change Staff Culture via Two Different Paths

Gene uses the metaphor of the train and Terry uses the metaphor of a community. Each talks about changing staff culture. Gene's train metaphor aptly reflects his concept that leaders move an organization forward:

> And when I first came I would say to some of the senior people: You know, look—a couple of things—everybody talks about this college as a finely tuned machine. What I'm seeing—as one of the most loyal, devoted, volunteers, passionate alumni—is it may be a finely tuned machine, but I think it's a Model T, and when I open the hood I see a lot of duct tape. [laughter] Okay? And we're being asked to go cross-country in the years to come [with this Model T]. And while this has served us extremely well and the Model T is one of the great inventions of all time—I'm not in any way saying that everything that we've done in the past is not good, is not wonderful—but we need to think about where we're going and how to get it done. And I don't think that this vehicle gets it done. I don't think that there are many more improvements that we can make to it. But you can't say that too loudly. I'm not trying to design a rocket ship here. We're going to get on a train. We're just going to build a train to begin with. But the thing is we have to do it, one, really fast, and two, keep enhancing it while it's moving. But the train is going to leave the station. Once it leaves the station, we'll make periodic stops to let people get on and let people get off. [laughter] I don't need

everybody driving the train. I'm happy to be the conductor or the person driving the train. But I can't do it by myself. I need a team of people, and together we're going to work together and we're going to decide how to do this for the university's long-term benefit that works with our culture, that's forward-looking but also respectful of our traditions, of the people who have poured out their lives and their jobs. But after sufficient warning, the train is leaving in four months. The train is leaving in three months. The train is leaving in 18 minutes. The train has to leave the station.

Gene situates himself as someone who supports the university and therefore as a reliable critic of his beloved institution. By suggesting the current Model T version of the institution needs to be replaced with a faster moving, more modern train, Gene introduces his vision of the future of the advancement office. This is precisely what he says a leader does.

Another critical element to Gene's idea of leadership is the notion of having a strategy to move the organization forward. Again, Gene's train analogy is a good representation of his strategy of continuous improvement. He says the train is always moving forward, just as he wants to see his organization move toward the idea of an optimized organization and away from the idea of a "mom and pop" shop. By setting the metaphors for the past advancement office culture in the 1920s, his call for change is more vibrant. Gene references his president's support of the goal to "modernize" the advancement office operation. This ties together his leadership perspective, his relationship to the university president, and his approach to the culture challenge.

Embedded in Gene's metaphor of the train is his concept of his mission. He says that becoming more like a train and less like a Model T will benefit the university in the long term and will balance the good of the past with the good of the future. Like several of his colleagues, Gene has worked with this staff to develop a set of guiding principles to explicitly reflect values he believes are important elements of the advancement office. He talks about helping staff members know when it is time to get off the train or how to be better travelers. He talks about the importance of hiring, training, performance management, assessment tools, and the role of HR as critical elements in his strategy for continuous improvement. He does not talk about using a consultant to help change the culture of his office. Gene's talk of changing culture helps provide insights into his concept of mission, his focus on his staff, his relationship to his president, and his perspective on leadership.

When Terry talks about her staff, she uses a distinctly different metaphor. As previously noted, Terry's mission filter, management-leadership lens, relationship to her president, and focus all revolve around building an institutional community dedicated to achieving the goals of the institution. She talks about "the ability to create a team, a sense of ownership, ownership for the staff, for the senior officers, for the organization and for the donors as well." The metaphor of creating a community conveys many of the values Terry says are most important to her.

Terry talks about achieving a "quite remarkable show of celebration and support and success—that is not so customary at [her university]." By contrasting the sense of joy she facilitated with the normal culture of her university, Terry positions her achievement of community as noteworthy: somehow, she overcame what others describe as the "weight of tradition." This remark also helps us appreciate the importance she places on praise and celebration as valued aspects of being in community.

Terry questions whether the "degree of intimacy and sense of family" she has facilitated during her tenure will be possible to achieve in the future when the need to outpace the prior year's fundraising goal is looming over the VP's head. She wonders whether the scale of the organization will make it possible for the VP "to even know a third of those people." Both of these remarks help convey Terry's emphasis on community.

"But I think another of the things that I think is complicated—with the big numbers and the big staffs—how do you create a welcoming ... a tolerance for creativity and entrepreneurship in these huge organizations?" Creativity and entrepreneurship are two additional important aspects of Terry's sense of community. She tells a story about how she saw an opportunity to leverage her institution's large number of loyal international alumni by creating a program directed to this constituency. She offers the story as an example of a time that she expressed creativity and entrepreneurship and found support for her ideas in a leadership that was potentially more willing to rely on their trust in her as a dedicated staff member rather than her ability to prove her idea using data. Relaying this story helps portray Terry's notion of community built on individual knowledge of each other and trust in each other's instincts. This puts her concern about organizational scale in perspective: In a less close knit culture, would she be able to achieve the same level of creativity and entrepreneurship?

Terry integrates the idea of constituents into her community metaphor. She talks about "one of the things that pleased me the most about the university's last campaign ... was how much the faculty liked it." This shows how much she values each member of the community and wants each member's enthusiastic commitment and support. She says that listening is the sign of both a good fundraiser and a good manager. And she talks about the value of ownership—this is, of owning one's actions. Terry conveys a clear idea of what it means to her to be a member of the community and illustrates her concept using examples from each aspect of her constituency.

Finally, Terry talks about the importance of integrity in a leader and illustrates what she means by using examples from each of the three presidencies she has experienced at her university. In a few of these stories, we can interpret her actions as those of the leader she describes. This tendency not to position herself as a leader seems related to her notion of her not taking much of an interest in management or organizations. She seems to be suggesting that her notion of organization as community worked for her but may no longer work or may no longer be a worthy model. In the following story, however, Terry demonstrates the integrity she says is characteristic of leaders and thus is enacting her form of leadership.

> **Interviewer: It sounds like you got people to change somehow.**
>
> Sometimes. Sometimes. You know one of the things that I think gets lost sometimes: one of the members of the board—one of the major donors—he and I fought like cats and dogs for a period of time. And at one of these farewell things he said that I had taught him everything that he knew about fundraising. And he said that we had fought all the time in the beginning. ... [W]hat he said was that when he came to be the chairman of the board that he thought that fundraising was just like sales—in fact, he insisted. And he said it's not. And I remember having this knock-down drag-out battle with him trying to say that in his industry the people that he was selling to NEEDED what he was selling. They didn't need to buy it from him. They could buy it from somebody else. But they needed in a timely way what he had to sell. And that was not true of philanthropy. So we finally got there one way or another. The real point isn't to educate the alumni you are going to see about our capital campaign. ... It isn't incumbent upon them to help us reach our goal.

Rather than quickly agree with me that she had in fact inspired people to change, she reflects that this happened "sometimes," not always. This is evidence of Terry being authentic and striving for accuracy—both aspects of integrity. She tells the story about the wealthy board member with whom she fought to illustrate her point that board members and fundraisers need to keep their roles in perspective relative to the other members of the community or institution. This story snippet demonstrates Terry acting with integrity. Even though her job is to raise money from wealthy donors, she remains true to herself by arguing with the board member about what she believes to be true. Once again we see her expressing concern for all members of the community.

The participant's choice of words to describe members of the organization conveys a sense of emotion. *Family, community,* and *constituent*: Each word conveys a different sense of the distance from speaker to organization. We hear, both in what Terry says and in the way that she says it, her emphasis on the importance of creating a sense of community across the broad spectrum of her constituency. In this we see her choosing a path to creating an organizational culture she values.

Sandy and Alex Preserve and Change Culture

Sandy and Alex talk about preserving certain aspects of institutional culture and changing others. There are several commonalities in their approaches and a few distinct differences. Comparing and contrasting their approaches across the broad spectrum of constituencies helps shed light on their leadership theories.

Sandy's words mirror her leadership theory. She says:

> But you know what we did there [at a previous university] and what I'm trying to do here [at her current university] is—you have to provide a stimulating environment with a lot of professional development and opportunities for people to grow. You know, titles and money, of course, is important. And you have to be competitive in terms of salary. You have to be competitive in terms of the titles that you are offering. But beyond that, people do look for other things. And it is the personal satisfaction that they get out of their jobs. It is the opportunity to make a difference. It is the opportunity to learn. It's being respected that counts more than—you know 5,000 dollars more in the paycheck. And that's something that one can build into the culture of an institution.

For Sandy, the best VPs see themselves in a service role. In the quote above, she describes providing the opportunity for people to find personal satisfaction in their jobs by giving them the opportunity to make a difference, to be of service. When asked what kind of a culture she wants to build, she ties it directly to her mission:

> What kind of a culture do I want to encourage? To me, again it goes back to what our purpose is. And it goes back to our foremost job being to develop those institutional relationships.

She explicitly cites several values that encourage developing institutional relationships, such as openness, transparency, creativity, diversity, and a desire to add value. In these snippets, we see Sandy performing her vision of leadership as service.

Here, Sandy links her organizational focus on the broad spectrum of constituencies, her mission, and her concept of leader being in a service role:

> To me what's important is to look at the individual that I am dealing with as he or she is today—with his or her needs, interests, opportunities, et cetera—and connect those to the institution. So that requires—now going back to institutional culture—that requires an openness within the culture. And many institutions have only begun to realize that we can't be silos.

She talks about achieving the culture she describes in several ways and across the spectrum. For example, she talks about "seamlessly plugging" donors into their areas of interest, regardless of who on her staff or who at the university is responsible for matching the donor with the interest. She talks about promoting extraordinarily good communication as an integral component of achieving a culture of openness. And her final and most important tip to achieving the culture she wants is to disregard structure.

> Don't care about structure. It doesn't matter who reports to whom. Just work with everybody as though they are on your staff. And that creates, over time, a sense of community. The other thing that I personally always and to this day have as a guiding light is: you have to add value to a relationship, so if you want to persuade somebody—a school, a program—to work with you, you won't achieve it by telling them they have to.

Whether talking about her staff, the faculty at the institution, or the donors, Sandy demonstrates that she disregards structure and looks for ways to add value. She talks about regularly convening a group of deans to discuss how her staff can be of service to the deans, and she talks about experimenting with different approaches until you find what works for a particular group. From Sandy's perspective, institutional relationships happen between donors and staff, staff and staff, as well as faculty and donors, to name just a few combinations. Sandy's focus on building relationships and adding value are demonstrations of her organizational focus, her mission filter, and her management-leadership lens acting together to guide her approach to the culture challenge.

Her approach to encouraging the culture she describes echoes her description of a good manager as well as a good leader. Sandy says a good manager has to recognize whom one can let loose and at the same time take responsibility to make sure things go well. She explains that she is the one ultimately accountable for success and failure. If she sees "something going in the wrong direction," she will "step in."

Sandy's holistic approach to preserving and changing institutional culture reveals the fuzzy lines between the members of the composite organization and the intertwining subcultures. Examining Sandy's approach suggests why some fundraisers talk about the profession as more of an "art" than a "science."

Alex's cultural goal is to act as the "keeper of the flame." Through this fitting metaphor, he conveys the deep respect he has for the institutional culture he says he inherited. His choice of words echoes his deep respect for the culture that "flourishes" at his university. He describes his challenge as introducing change in ways that preserves the existing collaboration and collegiality. He shares several stories that illustrate his concept of how effectively fundraisers and support staff share the kudos associated with raising large gifts. He talks about the need to quantify the concept of the "assist," much like in basketball where the team member passing the ball gets awarded an assist for helping score points. Unlike Sandy, he notes the role that budget and reporting structures play in different advancement office models. He notes the "forwardness, nimbleness, youthfulness" that he says are all part of the institutional culture. He conveys the respected role his office has at the institution by the following story:

> And this development office clearly under [previous VP's] tenure and even before has been the cavalry. And every time the place has needed something they come over the hill. So … that's part of it. This is an organization that is well valued around the campus. That in and of itself helps build the culture. Because people feel, "Hey, you know I'm making a contribution." So that's part of it.

Both Sandy and Alex define the culture challenge as introducing change in a way that honors the existing culture. The differences between the two can be found in the differences of the existing institutional environment.

In examining the first challenge, "Preserving or Changing Organizational Culture," the rich texture of the environment of higher education comes alive in the VPs' stories. Expectations of behavior as well as feelings about particular behaviors are woven into participant definitions and approaches

FIGURE 4. Culture Challenge

Dynamic interaction argument

VP's vision of leadership and institutional environment dynamically interacts with his or her definition and approach to changing organizational culture

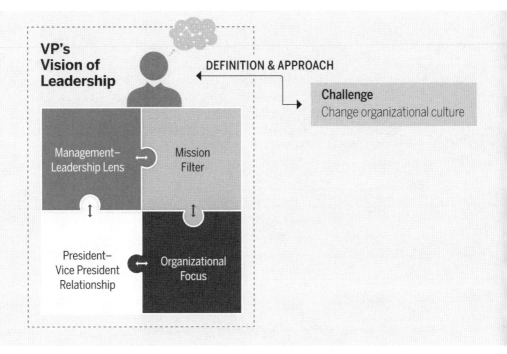

to culture. These accounts bring to life the often unspoken aspects of leading a change effort and touch on several aspects of culture warranting deeper research.[2] The importance of mission shines through in several VPs' stories of culture.

The culture challenge is not confined to advancement or higher education (Bensimon 1990; McLaughlin 2004; Pusser 2005). New school superintendents and principals often have to assess the local culture before making changes (Burdeno and Herrmann 2006; Cheever 1982). Volunteers serving as campaign chairs for local hospitals face similar dilemmas of managing culture while seeking financial support.

Using the Advancement Constellation as a map for approaching complex challenges encourages increased flexibility and creativity in decision making—but all of the examples are holistic. Consider Chris's advice to herself to go more slowly. What worked for Chris may not work for Jo. Nevertheless, these windows into the world of institutional advancement can provoke the student, the scholar, and the practitioner to consider his or her decision-making process relative to assessing organizational culture.

DEVELOPING LARGE GIFT STRATEGIES

According to one research firm, all of the institutions involved in this study raised gifts of $1 million in the last 20 years. However, only three of the 10 institutions raised a gift of $100 million, and each of these gifts was donated since 2000. Therefore, we see that raising a gift of $100 million is a relatively new phenomenon.

According to a prominent leadership theorist, a sign of the most difficult obstacle is the challenge of articulating the problem (Heifetz 1994). That is, the more difficult it is to articulate a problem, the more challenging the problem is. Using "difficulty of definition" as a guide, this section examines how the 10 participants articulate the problem of developing large gift strategies. Common elements emerge from the VPs' comments:

- The role of the staff,
- The need for a gift plan,
- The potential donor-university tension and
- The difficulty assessing achievement.

The sections that follow illustrate the complexity of this challenge and underscore the different approaches used by the participants to tackle the challenge. At the end of this section, one participant's story of raising a transformational gift serves as an exemplar of one approach.

Listening to the VPs identify what is problematic in developing large gift strategies will provide a broad view of the varying approaches to this challenge and will highlight the importance of each participant's leadership vantage point.

Role of the Staff

From a composite perspective of the participants, the term *staff* refers to the president, the VP, the large gift fundraiser, as well as faculty, deans, and senior staff members.

As previously mentioned, several vice presidents describe the president's ability to build relationships with potential wealthy donors as critical to the strategy of raising such large gifts. If the president is not interested or not suited to developing a relationship with the prospective donor, then creating a strategy is described as problematic. Another critical function of the president relative to large gift strategies is the clarity with which the president articulates the priorities of the university and the degree to which the president perceives that he or she is responsible for deciding on fundraising investments. Several VPs talked about the difficulty of achieving an appropriate balance of the president's time, given all his or her other demands.

Some VPs perceive the vice president's responsibility to be the senior fundraiser of the institution and thus intimately involved in the largest gift development strategies. These folks argue that the vice president has greatest access to the key decision-makers and knowledge of important new projects—both critical to the successful development of the largest gifts. By virtue of attending senior staff meetings and working closely with the deans, the argument continues, the VP serves as the model fundraiser for the faculty and deans. Strong fundraising credibility is needed to forge the agreements critical to large gifts. Alex expresses this idea when he says that "my credibility is at risk if I can't say, 'You know what? Last week the president and I saw So and So and we were engaged in a conversation about the following three things.'" In direct contrast, others explicitly state large gift fundraising is not the main part of the VP's job. Thus, while a president's role in large gift fundraising can be potentially problematic, the VP's understanding of his or her responsibilities relative to the challenge can also contribute to the difficulty of developing a large gift strategy.

Many participants agree that the fundraisers involved in large gift development need to be focused on building the relationship with the prospect, need to understand the priorities of the university, need incentives to share the gift strategies across multiple schools at the university, and need to be exposed to good mentoring. Some VPs expressed an interest in mentoring new fundraisers themselves. Most participants acknowledge this to be a tall order to fill. They say there are not enough good fundraisers available to hire and there isn't enough time for fundraisers to do the many steps mentioned above.

In talking about managing large gift development strategies, participants agree that there is more at play than the credibility of the VP. Some participants attribute a common view of fundraisers as "party throwers" or "frivolous" to the relative youth of the profession; others suggest the lack of credentialing is another reason the profession is perceived as not as challenging as other roles at the university. All of the participants talk in some fashion about the importance of including faculty and senior staff in the development of large gifts—and also about how engaging faculty and staff is more complicated when fundraisers do not have adequate credibility.

Clarifying the role of the president, the role of the VP, and the role of non-fundraising senior staff in the gift strategies seems key to all participants. Developing credibility of the fundraising staff internally and externally is essential as well. And finally, addressing a means of gaining access to information about priorities and possibilities is another crucial element.

Need for a Gift Plan

Chris wonders whether institutions have the capacity to plan for developing very, very large gifts. She articulates her concerns as follows:

> One of the other biggest capacities that we're still lacking here … that I think hurts our fundraising a lot … is that we don't have a capacity to plan for very, very large gifts. I think when I look at how many 100 million dollar gifts are going to all of these other organizations and we are rarely on that list … that it … it just seems ridiculous! [laughter] … That we have a donor who wants to … is thinking about a 100 million dollar gift … we can't come up with a plan. Well, what are we going to do university-wide? Well, what would we do with 100 million dollars? So it seems just … it's a huge capacity that's missing. And it doesn't belong in development … but we're the ones who suffer, I think, by not having it, because our donors say, "Well, how come you're not on that list more often—at [the] 100 million dollar gift level?" and we don't have a way … a structure. … So what if we have a university-wide center for [X]? Who does it report to? How does it function? Where do the appointments get made? How do the faculty get tenure? It's just really hard. But we need … that is absolutely essential that we crack that nut.

Chris's description of planning capacity highlights several critical tensions. First, she says that one of the biggest obstacles is posed by the very structure of the organization responsible for matching the gift to the institution. She says that no one is responsible for creating such a vision or for bringing it to fruition. Chris suggests that a person and a unit within the institution need to be identified to create such an intricate gift plan. She also identifies components of the plan that will make creating the plan challenging: determining reporting structures, resolving functions, defining the appointment processes, and agreeing upon the tenure processes. Chris gives an example of a donor who is ready to make a very, very large gift but the institution is unable to provide a description of how the donor's investment will be implemented. Thus, Chris talks about clarifying the role of the staff but also about organizational structures and plans. In this quotation, we see how Chris's view of institutional governance guides her definition of the large gift challenge.

Furthermore, in this snippet, Chris's sense of agency, her belief that her role is to manage effectively rather than be the "senior fundraiser," her role of balancing her president, and her organizational focus contribute to her recommendation to define a structure for enacting the planning component of raising large gifts. She references other institutions that are getting large gifts and thus conveys that it is possible to get such a gift. In this way, we know that her proposal addresses thorny but resolvable questions.

Chris's blended management-leadership lens that emphasizes both good management and good leadership and her view of institutional governance informs her approach to this challenge. Unlike Sandy's concept that structure does not matter, Chris's talk emphasizes those aspects of management that are concerned with the structure of responsibilities. Chris describes her mission of raising the maximum money possible for the university through making the structures work.

Regardless of who is responsible for creating a gift plan, all of the VPs seem to agree that such a plan is critical for raising very, very large gifts. Thus, the VP's vantage point drives the way each envisions the creation of the gift plan and the degree to which the gift plan is influenced by the current structures of the university.

Several participants extend the definition of the problem from the need for a gift plan to the need to marry the gift plan to the institution's long-term strategy. In some cases, the participants say that the lack of clear university strategies complicates the large gift challenge. Some say that if the strategies are not written down, confusion may enter the process of aligning the gift plan with university priorities. They note that if the priorities were not collectively reached, some of the constituents may not enthusiastically support the implementation of a very large gift plan or—worse—may actively work against such an implementation. At other times, the participants say the problem involves the donor's desires not matching the existing university strategies and the difficulty of compromising in a way that benefits both the donor and the university. Some describe the silo nature of institutions and the inherent conflicts in resolving differences between multiple competing perspectives. Some attribute this characteristic at their institutions to the structure of their funding models, while others suggest the institutional culture is the source of the problem. Finally, some participants question the need for a campaign as a means of motivating such very, very large gifts, while others believe that campaigns are part of the motivation process. Most of the VPs mentioned the importance of the financial structure and especially the role of the vice president of finance[3] in participating in many of the decisions Chris identifies above.

The different approaches to creating a gift plan emphasize the importance of the VP's vantage point. Best practices do not necessarily apply across different advancement landscapes. Instead, these different approaches emphasize the importance of flexible and creative decision-making as a key contributor to successful advancement leadership.

Potential Donor-University Tension

None of the participants describes a lack of potential donors as particularly challenging; rather, as noted above, many say it is sometimes difficult to align potential donors with university priorities. Some participants note that an increasing number of donors consider contributions as investments. They say that when donations are viewed as investments, donors often want to manage the relationship quite closely, and this situation may produce competing objectives. Some participants describe the donor-institution tension as being related to disagreement about the integrity of the donor.

Sometimes VPs consider the challenge of creating this donor-institution relationship to be one of the most satisfying aspects of the job because it makes one stretch. Sandy's leadership theory resounds in her approach to this aspect of large gift fundraising. She says:

> I think in development more than anywhere else that you are a servant of people. And I use that word advisedly. You serve the institution and you serve the donors. And there are wonderful opportunities in there, even for your own personal development. Because it forces you—if you take it seriously—it forces you to look for the best in people where sometimes, if you weren't in that position, you might just see something that's not that terrific.

Sandy talks about the challenge of connecting the donor with the institution as one of the exciting aspects of philanthropy.

Difficulty Assessing Achievement

In many ways the difficulties of assessing success for large gifts is a subset of the overall challenge described in Challenge 3, "Assessing Success." However, certain complications are potentially unique to large gift development. For example, many participants point to the concept of raising money for the long-term as one of the key hurdles. They say this makes assessing the process and the results different from assessment criteria used in the for-profit world. Some say the business metaphor of marketing maps nicely to the advancement functions in higher education, while others strongly disagree. Several talk about the many hands contributing to the raising of such large gifts. How does one reward all the people who helped to make such a gift possible? If one rewards only those most directly connected to the process, then how will collaboration be affected?

As we have seen elsewhere in this book, the answers to these nuanced questions seem directly tied to the vantage point of the VP. The varying perspectives on assessing success are illustrated in more detail in Challenge 3.

Sean's Story of Raising a $100 Million Gift

Sean's story shows him encouraging a potential donor who others thought would not be able to or willing to give to the university.

> Early on we got [a very large gift—over $100 million] from one donor. It's our biggest gift ever. He gave three very large gifts, all in a period of about a year and half. And there will be more there because he set up … He had dropped out of [the university] so I'm not going to go through it. But I made a cold call on him.

The details that Sean provides help portray him as his definition of a leader. According to Sean's theory, a leader inspires people to reach beyond their self-imposed limitations. The description of the very generous donor's background positions the donor as someone unlikely to be able to give such a large gift. The fact that he didn't graduate from the university also adds to the idea that he might not be as inclined to give as alumni who attend the full four years. Finally, the fact that Sean mentions this was a "cold call," as opposed to a solicitation over a long period of time and with several other staff members involved, helps to show Sean as a person who goes beyond normal expectations. By choosing to tell this story, Sean situates himself as an exemplar of his definition of a good leader relative to his institution and this challenge.

Sean describes working with members of the board of trustees as well as senior staff to convince them that the gift meets the university gift guidelines. Sean's account positions him as an experienced fundraiser who is able to leverage his past successes and failures. Being able to offer experience and good judgment are two characteristics that Sean describes in a good manager. Thus, the details of this story show Sean acting out his definition of a good manager and demonstrating his blended management-leadership lens.

Sean's impetus to tell the story comes in answer to a question about his institution's recent surge. Sean attributes the institution's success to the solicitation and receipt of this very large gift. This correlates nicely with Sean's sense of mission: "the greatest measure of success is using your fundraising abilities to meet the institution's goals." As previously mentioned, Sean sees his president as a critical element of the fundraising process, and Sean talks about how he leveraged her meeting the very generous donor. Sean also talks about working with the VP of finance to help her understand the complicated aspects of the gift and to forge a consistent understanding of how the gift helps the institution achieve its financial goals. Finally, Sean's organizational focus facing this institutional challenge encompasses a previous nondonor, his staff, the university president, the vice president of finance, the trustees, and the students—the broad spectrum. Sean's story of raising a very large gift provides just one holistic approach to this challenge and simultaneously reveals deeper insights into his leadership theory.

Challenge 2, "Developing Large Gift Strategies," focuses on exploring several common thorny dimensions of developing very large gifts. The participants' stories demonstrate their shared concerns with the role of the institutional president, their own role, the quality of staff, and the amount of time needed.

Chris's focus on creating the capacity to plan for such large gifts offers one concrete path and reflects her leadership theory as well as her perspective on institutional governance. A snippet from Sandy's approach to large gift development reflects her concept of leadership as service. Despite the differences in their approaches, we can glean the importance of addressing roles and plans as part of any advancement leader's approach to seeking the largest contributions.

FIGURE 5. Transformational Gift Challenge

Dynamic interaction argument

VP's vision of leadership and institutional environment dynamically interacts with his or her definition and approach to raising transformational gifts

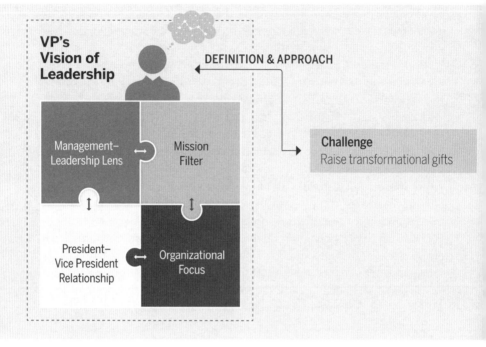

Challenge 2 introduces potential conflicts in assessing success of large gift development. If success assessment strategies are misaligned with the VP's vantage point and environment, then the overall chance to reach the transformation goal is jeopardized. Concrete stories in the next section will illustrate the beauty and the dangers.

Finally, Sean's story illustrates one holistic approach to the nuances of raising large gifts, exemplifies potential donor-university tensions, and demonstrates his leadership theory.

Most VPs emphasize having a clear vision of the institutional priorities, whether this vision is written in the form of a strategic plan or shared verbally. Such clarity of vision is often seen as a key element of leadership (Bennis and Nanus 2003; Kotter 2002; Williams 2005). Reviewing the holistic approaches offered in these stories in light of one's own vantage point opens the doors to flexible and creative decision-making.

Through the stories in this section, we see the VPs' differing visions of leadership dynamically interact with their varied approaches to developing gift strategies. They do not all place the same importance on marrying the donor's vision to the institutional vision. Nor do they all advocate for a structured implementation plan that will address the complexities entailed in raising such large gifts. They choose paths that suit their visions, their institutions, and their external circumstances. Yet the common questions they ask are useful guideposts for advancement leaders facing the challenge of raising the largest gifts.

Challenge 3

ASSESSING SUCCESS

Almost all the vice presidents reference the "bottom line" of fundraising as a quantifiable measure of money raised. Frequently the way the participants talk implies that this bottom line is an easy answer for assessing success, but not the only answer. Each participant references the tension between the ease with which a vice president can point to the amount of money raised for a given year and all of the aspects of success that are not addressed when one doesn't look beyond this one easy measure.

By examining what makes assessment complicated for each vice president, the participant's leadership vantage point is revealed.

More Complicated Than It Seems

Not surprisingly, several VPs talk about the importance of having a clear vision of success prior to trying to assess success. For Pat, this relates to the institution's leaders working together to articulate a plan and then flowing gift strategies and success assessment criteria from that plan. Jordan talks about "winning the campaign on paper first" and the way that the paper plan keeps staff focused on achieving success. As mentioned in the previous section, participants talk about the complications of articulating a vision and sharing that vision across multiple audiences. Pat, Sandy, Alex, and Jo all note that the plan or vision needs to be squarely focused on the institution's future and describe the challenge of assessing success that may not be visible for many years. Almost all the participants discuss the lack of standard, comprehensive, and agreed-upon assessment criteria. They say the lack of standards makes gaining agreement on investment strategies more difficult. A few point to a lack of accountability across higher education as a rationale for the lack of agreement about assessment criteria. Some argue that measuring collaboration and relationship building destroys the authenticity of both. All participants agree that the specific culture of the institution plays a significant role in assessing success and is sometimes the biggest stumbling block.

Sandy Talks About Success

It doesn't mean what you might expect, i.e., the millions of dollars raised or so. Success really to me means the building of meaningful relationships with individuals—not necessarily to me, but building relationships to the institution that then endure regardless of, you know, whether I am there or not. I think that's real success. To make people feel enriched after they have made gifts to an institution. To make people feel that they are part of the institution—that they have a role there—that it's part of their lives. That's how I measure success.

Sandy's perspective on success is firmly planted on the cornerstones of her leadership theory: choice of focus, management-leadership lens, role of president, and mission. As described earlier, Sandy's focus is the broad spectrum of constituents. She describes building relationships of donors to the institution as represented by the president, the faculty, the students, the other alumni, and the staff. Success is a direct answer to fulfilling her mission to provide the financial resources for the university to accomplish its goals. In the following quote describing success, Sandy demonstrates that she relies on her intuition to help assess success, thus setting the stage for the subsequent quote in which she shows that she fulfills her definition of a good manager as well as a good leader.

Well I mean you know it requires that you are very much in touch with your audience, with your alumni, with your donors, with your friends. And then you get the feeling. It shows itself—it manifests itself by, you know, you have a job to do and you ask for volunteers, and if you have more volunteers volunteering than you need that's an indication that people have a good relationship. It's the, you know, day-to-day interactions with people that shows you their willingness, their eagerness to be part of what you are doing. There's no metrics to measure it—that's true. But you know when it's there.

… And that is the trend toward metrics/measurements et cetera. Now mind you, I am very committed to metrics and measurements and productivity measurements and all that. But what I see happening is that we are building poor models. That may work when you sell widgets but completely ignores the fact that what we are doing is basically developing meaningful relationships. And to count how many visits somebody makes or set goals of how many visits somebody needs to make has a lot of unintended consequences. You go away and get the easy visits to make your quota and you go out and it's always you who visits—even though it might be the right thing to do for a faculty member to visit or to bring somebody else in. It has a lot of downsides that people don't think about. ... And just because it looks great that you can measure it.

According to Sandy, a manager has to take responsibility and accountability to make sure things go well. Sandy's sense of agency is apparent in the following words: "you know when it's there." This simple statement is one indication of her taking responsibility for knowing when the job has been done well. Some of her colleagues refer to this sense of knowing as experience or good judgment. In the second quote above, she points out the dangers of measuring and holding staff accountable based on the wrong metrics.

These snippets help us understand Sandy's concept of the service nature of leadership, her strong sense of mission, and her view of a manager's need to be accountable. In addition, her narratives offer one way to define the success assessment challenge by being in touch with one's audience and relying on more qualitative indicators of success.

Pat Talks About Success

Pat's theory of leadership explicitly links vision, mission, and success. Her theory places personal success second to the organization's success. She says that she speaks about the organization's success to all members of the constituency, including the president. In her remarks below, Pat describes what she considers one of the most difficult aspects of defining success:

> The real complexity in all of this is mapping it back to the institution itself. ... Frankly, while we're right on target in terms of the campaign, ... we're exactly where we should be and that's all good. I still think that we should be raising much more money than we are. And I know that we've ... we've gone through five years of some real hurdles institutionally ... some really tough, tough times. And so how else do we evaluate our success in moving through those hurdles?

Throughout her interview Pat has spoken quickly and without hesitation on most topics. In the excerpt above, the hesitation in Pat's talk shows that she is thinking hard about what she is saying, wrestling with the ideas. The tough times she mentions have to do with the university locale struggling with a very troubling experience. In her final remarks, Pat draws attention to intertwining the specific culture of the university, the institution's particular history, and the ability to determine what facilitates success as well as how to evaluate success. These remarks bring to light Pat striving to fulfill her definition of both a good manager and a good leader. She says a good manager puts in place structures and principles to facilitate her vision of success. Yet in these final remarks, Pat talks about situations that occur in the local environment—factors outside her purview as a manager but within her scope as a leader. She says that the challenge of evaluating success while moving through hurdles or events specific to her particular institution is something that she "struggles with as a leader." In this simple statement, Pat refines her definition of what it means to put personal success second to the organization and what it means to "guide the conduct of the organization." This short narrative offers insights to like-minded practitioners and provides an example of the dynamic interaction of institution, external factors, and individual leadership theory.

A subtitle of this challenge might be to "be careful what you wish for," since measuring and rewarding only dollars raised might disrupt the organization from achieving its complete mission. Especially in times of severe economic constraint, aligning leadership vantage point, institutional assessment strategies, and success calls for increased attention. The dynamic interaction model offers a tangible means for a financial leader to examine his or her vantage point in the light of a particular institutional environment. By clearly understanding one's own vantage point, one is better positioned to think flexibly about options for assessing the success of oneself and one's organization and, in this way, to preserve an authentic commitment to "something bigger than ourselves."

FIGURE 6. Success Challenge

Dynamic interaction argument

VP's vision of leadership and institutional environment dynamically interacts with his or her definition and approach to assessing success

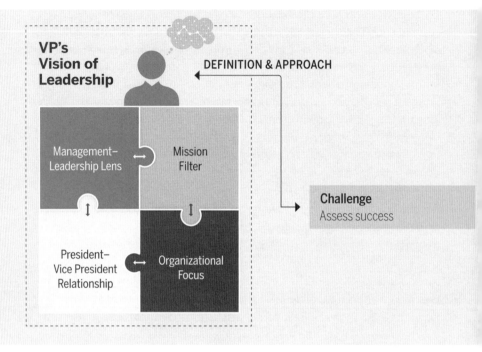

IMPLICATIONS OF THE ADVANCEMENT CONSTELLATION

Despite sharing similar challenges, the 10 advancement leaders in our study manage the hurdles differently. They don't agree on assessment strategies beyond the "bottom line." Some want to preserve culture, while others want to change culture. They all want to raise large gifts yet no one has found the best practice. Instead, throughout chapter 2, we have seen the importance of aligning vantage point with challenge. We hear important questions to ask regarding each challenge, and we are reminded that the answers to these questions need to be adapted to the particular advancement landscape.

Accepting the proposed Advancement Constellation has several implications. As many vice presidents noted in chapter 2—and their observations are supported by research (CASE InfoCenter 2008; Drozdowski 2004; Joslyn, Berkshire, and Quotah 2009)—graduate level fundraising programs are limited. In troubled economic times, research indicates, already small professional development budgets are cut more extensively (Joslyn, Berkshire, and Quotah 2009). As an alternative or as a supplement to professional advancement programs, the 10 cases described in this study provide accessible reference for students, faculty, and practitioners. The student gains a framework for thinking about the dilemmas facing advancement leaders. The faculty teaching advancement benefit from a viable framework for helping students disentangle the nuances of advancement work and glean several robust cases illustrating the framework. Finally, the practitioner gains an elegant way of thinking about messy problems with multiple moving parts. Given the importance of advancement work, the growing nonprofit leadership gap (Joslyn, Berkshire, and Quotah 2009), and the dynamic interaction of leadership visions with environments and challenges, a case-based approach to developing future advancement decision-making skills is a promising means of strengthening the field.

As an example of broadening the applicability of the dynamic interaction model, consider that long-term budgetary shortfalls and government programs are encouraging school superintendents to seek private sector investment through Public Private Partnerships (PPP) and venture philanthropy ("New Future" 2008). Clearly, managing the public education mission amid growing broad-based constituencies including a PPP presents increased challenges to the leadership team. Using the Advancement Constellation provides school superintendents a framework for considering important challenges that may be new to those leaders unfamiliar with advancing philanthropic pursuits.

In addition to being applicable to the development of future advancement leaders and to new entrants into the field of philanthropy, the model affords help to public universities unfamiliar with cultivating resources. The downturn in the economy caused more public universities within the United States and abroad to turn to philanthropists to help minimize the gap between available resources and requirements needed to educate tomorrow's citizens. As several VPs noted, today's advancement leaders are sowing the seeds for the future. The Advancement Constellation offers an approach for board members, university presidents, and others to consider the questions of fit. Rather than recruit new VPs by simply using a qualifications and trait-based approach, the dynamic interaction model implies the need to focus on "fit" of the candidate's vantage point with current university challenges and environment.

Closely related to recruiting is executive coaching. For similar reasons, those who advise advancement leaders need to consider the dynamic interaction of individual leadership vision, current institution, and particular significant challenges. By coaching nonprofit leaders to consider their vantage point relative to their institution and significant hurdle, the coach helps the leader increase outcome options and develops flexible decision-making skills. Both are deemed important by several outstanding leadership researchers (Burns 1979; Heifetz 1994; Helsing et al. 2008; Wheatley 2006; Williams 2005).

In difficult economic circumstances, some leaders turn to fundraising as means of increasing revenue, while others contemplate downsizing advancement organizations. When considering cutbacks, the importance of balance and fit can be overlooked. The Advancement Constellation provides leaders a means to adjust budgets *and* strategically envision the future. The "belt tightening" challenge becomes an opportunity to optimize the fit of leader, environment, and demanding problem.

As some participants noted, applying rigid or unrefined assessment strategies without due consideration of the constituency and the goals might have unintended results. Whether using the aid of a coach or reflecting by oneself, the diversity of approaches offers the practitioner concrete examples of flexible mental modeling. As eloquently described by Bolman and Deal (2003), such flexibility increases one's ability to find creative solutions to tough challenges. Perhaps more important than the diverse tangible exemplars, chapter 2 underscores the importance of considering the holistic model when approaching questions that don't have easy answers. By grasping and acknowledging one's vantage point, one can consider alternatives in developing approaches and thus create possibilities.

In addition to having implications for the nuances of advancement work, this study has implications for future research. Participants' discussions of the complexity of the environment, in addition to existing research (Julius, Baldridge, and Pfeffer 1999; Pfeffer 1992; Pusser 2003), suggests deeper consideration of the relevance of political processes to the work of the advancement leader. As noted earlier, several vice presidents reference the importance of ethics in changing culture or seeking large gifts. One very well-known political historian and leadership expert, James McGregor Burns, coined the term *transformational leader* to describe the leader who relies on positive politics to achieve important ends (Burns 1979, 2003). Given the subtleties of fundraising, as shown in the participants' cases, and the value many place on integrity in their roles, an exploration of the politics of ethical advancement warrants more study.

Closely related to the examination of ethics is the investigation of the rhetoric of advancement. *Rhetoric* is defined here as "the art or study of using language effectively and persuasively" (American Heritage, 2004). The negotiating, timing, framing, information analysis, interest articulation, and interpersonal influence involved in advancement work all rely on communication as meaning making. Using language to make meaning—or envision paths to the future—is both subtle and necessary for nonprofit leaders to master (Booth 2004; Grunig et al. 2000; Schiffrin 2006). The participants in this study didn't necessarily talk about rhetoric as integral to the work of advancement, yet another investigation of these same interviews might prove or disprove the relevance of such an analysis.

Finally, researching other members of the advancement constituent map is another possibility for future investigation. Given the scope of this study, none of the participants' constituents were interviewed. This initial study suggests exploring organizational well-being is well served by examining the interaction of the leader's choice of organizational focus, concept of culture, assessment strategies, and constituent perspectives.

At a minimum, I hope that chapter 2, "Fitting Vantage Point with Challenge," prompts lively debate about the varying perspectives on successful advancement leadership and the viability of the proposed model.

NOTES

1. Pseudonym for the institution's president.

2. Several researchers have written about the connection between culture and leadership decision making (Bensimon 1990; Bensimon and Neumann 1993, 2000; Pusser 2003; Cameron and Quinn 2011; Hofstede and Hofstede 2005). In light of the increased research on culture, the VP interviews in this study deserve further investigation and consideration of the role of culture in the advancement leader's decision-making process.

3. Typically, the VP of Finance is responsible for overseeing budget and planning, cash management, disbursements, grants and contracts, as well as student financial services. This role focuses on managing spending rather than soliciting funds.

CHAPTER 3

ADVISING
PROSPECTIVE ADVANCEMENT LEADERS

Despite the differing vantage points of the vice presidents, their collective wisdom offers insights that span institutional environment and various difficult challenges. The chart on page 90 summarizes the participants' responses to my direct question about advice they might give to new vice presidents and my distillation of their remarks about underlying principles important to success.

The goal of this section is to capture and illustrate this collective wisdom as succinctly as possible. Examples throughout this section serve to clarify their perspectives. As a whole, chapter 3 emphasizes self-awareness as a means to developing one's individual leadership theory.

Know How You Fit

This area of advice from the VPs has multiple strands, all of which build on knowing oneself and the institution. Matching one's skills, values, and passions to the institution is integral to envisioning advancement leadership. Throughout this study, participants' perceptions of institutional culture and leadership theories vary. If I have convinced my reader, then Lee's advice to exercise due diligence in assessing one's fit for the environment will ring true:

> Well, I think first and foremost: absolute due diligence before you become the VP is critical. And the more you can garner perspective on the job from trustees, from faculty, from leadership, from staff—either directly or indirectly, from current or former—I think is critical. So that first and foremost. To try to really understand what's the culture that you're entering into. And then I think the assessment of whether or not you can have an impact.

COLLECTIVE WISDOM

Know how you fit

Exercise due diligence in making tough decisions
Match your skills, values and passion to the institution
Know your strengths and your weaknesses
Distinguish between role and self

Develop partners

Get external perspectives
Develop trust
Build relationships

Listen
Balance
Be passionate
Keep a sense of humor

Lee's use of the words *absolute* and *critical* underlines how important he considers this piece of advice. It implies a need to be self-reflective, since being able to use the second part—the notion of assessing one's ability to impact the institution via the role—requires knowing one's leadership theory.

Elsewhere, Jordan echoes Lee's counsel to a certain extent when he says it is important to "match" or fit oneself to a particular organization. Lee and Jordan both imply that the values emphasized at each institution differ, and both either imply or state concretely elsewhere that a prospective vice president needs to be clear about his or her value system.

What shines through in the stories of all the VPs is that they ascribe the difference in values to a combination of the history of the institution, the location of the institution, the current president of the institution, and the values the advancement vice president emphasizes. One participant talks about the downsides of assuming a role without having thought first about the type of "persona" that the new role requires. She describes how in her past role she was very much a manager and a facilitator. She says her boss was the leader and set the tone. In her new role as vice president, she describes her current boss as being very different than her prior boss and says she needs to "balance" the views of her president in forming her plans for her role. Thinking about one's persona in such flexible ways is akin to understanding one's role and knowing if the role is a comfortable fit.

Pat talks about the importance of seeking feedback on one's performance—a way to gain an increased understanding of one's strengths and weaknesses relative to the role. Like many of her colleagues, Pat describes using a professional coach to help a new vice president understand the requirements of the new role and to understand how the new vice president's current skills and values align with the new role. From Pat's perspective, making the transition from being a manager to being a leader is one of the hardest transitions. Unlike others who see the two lenses as tightly connected, Pat talks about the leadership lens as distinctly different from the management lens. Pat describes the importance of constraining herself from perfecting a gift proposal to enable staff to make the proposal and to learn from whatever mistakes might be made. Several of the participants talked about the importance of mistakes as an integral aspect of self-knowledge and growth, both their own growth and the growth of staff members.

Gene is another participant who offers self-reflection as an important aspect of grappling with the questions of leadership, success, and organizational well-being. He says he regularly asks himself, "Why do I do this?" For him, part of the answer entails personal growth and development. Again, this advice implies awareness of one's strengths and weaknesses as being important to success. In order to grow as a leader, one needs to articulate how one thinks about both leadership and success.

Sandy advises: "When you deal with people who have a lot of money, you have to be grounded yourself." Terry elaborates Sandy's remarks about being grounded when she talks about the importance of distinguishing one's role as vice president from one's self. Several of the participants talk about the importance of remembering that the goal of the vice president is to foster a meaningful relationship between the donor and the institution as represented by the faculty, the president, the students, or a member of the advancement staff. Alex says it is important to remember at the end of the day that he goes home to his house. Terry goes on to elaborate the significance of keeping the role and value of fundraising at the institution in perspective.

> And I think one of the things that is important to me is that the fundraising organization knows its place. Knows what it is and how important it is. And also knows what it isn't. And sometimes over the years I would get worried that some of the people on our staff—if you gave them a ranking of the departments, of the functions at the university—would rank resource development before admissions and financial aid.

Terry's comments about the role of fundraising at the institution help clarify Sandy's remarks about the importance of a vice president being grounded. Being grounded, exercising due diligence, matching self to institution, knowing one's strengths and weaknesses combine to form the strongest advice participants offer a new vice president: know yourself. Considering this strong advice in light of this study's argument—observing and understanding the dynamic interaction of one's leadership theory, institutional environment, and significant challenges in forming one's leadership approach—suggests that vice presidents should build time in their schedules for self-reflection.

Develop Partners

Having trusted advisers is critical. Like Pat, Jo talks about the support she offers for those senior staff members who seek professional coaching. Her remarks emphasize the need to hear diverse perspectives and to interact with someone who is willing and able to challenge the vice president's thinking. Sandy says diverse opinions make one's thinking stronger. Some VPs like Jordan ask staff to do this for them but acknowledge the difficulty that direct reports might have in freely offering constructive criticism of the boss's thinking. Several colleagues recommend seeking advice from trustees because it serves the dual purpose of building a meaningful relationship and gaining a needed external perspective.

Several participants discuss the importance of trust. Alex advises that one's success is directly linked with one's credibility. Alex and others talk about acting in ways that engender trust. Alex says being an honest broker lays the foundation for being trusted. Lee talks about this concept as transparency and notes that it is one of his core principles. Sean says a leader needs to be predictable. Each of these participants is describing trustworthiness and the importance of trust in a meaningful relationship. As seen in Alex's remarks as well as argued throughout this study, almost every one of the vice presidents advocates for the importance of building relationships with the vice president's constituents. The trusted adviser relationship is a special type of relationship, and many of the principles that the participants say are critical to building a constituent relationship are also found in the trusted adviser relationship.

Listen

Closely related to the ability to develop trusted advisers is Terry's advice to cultivate and reward the ability to listen to one's self and to others. This seems connected to the ability to know one's strengths and weaknesses as well as to keep one's mind flexible. Terry says the fundraiser's role is to listen carefully to where the donor's interests and the university's needs intersect. Sandy describes listening as letting go of one's personal ego. Lee talks about going to each senior staff member's office within a short time of his arrival at his university and saying to new colleagues, "I'm here to listen to what you want. Tell me what you think that you need. What are the barriers to that?"

Balance

Jo's metaphor of the seesaw captures the balancing act she describes as being part of many significant choices. As mentioned earlier, Chris talks about a good manager balancing the many tasks on her plate and, later, about how she realizes her actions need to balance her president's actions. Pat and Jordan talk about balancing the ability to focus on one's vision with the ability to think flexibly. Jordan also talks about balancing his president. One of the major balancing acts Jordan describes is the difficulty of encouraging his staff to balance work life with home life—not asking them to solely devote themselves to the job. In Challenge 1, several participants talk about the need for balancing new principles and new values with past values. This might also be seen as pacing change according to the culture's ability to productively work with the change. Terry talks about the need to balance the intimacy of the advancement office with the size of the staff required to accomplish the mission. Recognizing the seesaw and learning to balance it is inherent in many participants' description of leadership.

Be Passionate

Several of the participants talk about being passionate. Pat and Jordan both say it is a critical aspect of leadership. Gene describes himself as one of the most loyal and passionate graduates of his university. And Sandy provides the following insight when she talks about good development officers:

> Part of what it means to be a development officer has to be a natural curiosity about the world around you. And the world around you at a university is so exciting. That's another point that makes a good development officer—you just have to be passionate about what a place is doing. You can't expect a person to be passionate about every single thing that is going on, but the advancement of knowledge, the scientific discoveries … if you are not excited about those and feeling great to be at a place where these things are happening, then I think, well, forget it—you shouldn't be in the position.

The stories, words and faces of the vice presidents in this study all reveal their commitment and dedication to their philanthropic mission.

Keep a Sense of Humor

Closely related to passion is humor. The ability to maintain a sense of humor, in spite of the long hours, frequent crises, and significant challenges, is critical to a vice president. Jordan articulates this "as waking up most days eager to get to work." Sean talks about truly enjoying the job. Sandy says that being an advancement vice president forces a person to look for the best in other people and to grow in ways that you might not otherwise grow.

The most fruitful way to leverage the collective wisdom presented in this book is with a strong understanding of one's own vision of leadership, institution, and significant challenges. Self-awareness means knowing one's own point of view and how that can be considered when developing one's leadership vision relative to one's environment. Hopefully, these nuggets of wisdom from the participants serve to reinforce the reader's own good instincts and stimulate consideration of old problems from new vantage points.

 CHAPTER 4

APPLYING
THE ADVANCEMENT
CONSTELLATION

Envisioning advancement leadership is a personal journey within a particular institutional landscape at a particular moment in time. There are many ways to apply this work, depending on who you are, where you are, and when you are.

Advancement Executive

Your title may be executive director or CEO or alumni affairs director or even vice president of advancement. In any of these cases, your role has a great similarity to that of the 10 VPs interviewed in this study. Depending on the length of time you've been in your role, you can use the Advancement Constellation as a checklist to build or review your leadership vision. You can refine your own leadership cornerstones through comparison with the snippets provided in chapter 1. Clarifying your own definition of the constellation building blocks may help you crystallize an approach to a challenge. Any one of the building blocks or all four of them could form the basis of an off-site meeting with your senior team members or with your board of directors. Clarification of your own vision and improved communication with those around you are key benefits of applying the Advancement Constellation. Since the approach does not suggest a proscribed leadership style but rather encourages self-reflection, the framework facilitates dialogue.

Examining fit might be a growth step for you within your current institution or an option for your exploration of a new path. *Fit* might reference your relationship to your president or the chairperson of your board or the "owner" of your foundation. On the other hand, exploring fit might involve looking at how your concept of leadership and perspective on governance meshes with the particulars of your institution. Given the number of moving parts in the Advancement Constellation, examining fit might be considered on an annual basis as a means to help you adjust to the current environment and challenges.

The prospective advancement leader benefits from striving to find a good fit with the institutional president. The 10 vice presidents in this study spoke openly about the potential pitfalls inherent in this critical relationship. What do you want in your relationship to your president? Contrast what *you* want with the relationships represented by each of the 10 VPs. Consider using the questions outlined in chapter 1 on the many facets of the president–vice president relationship prior to interviewing for an advancement leadership position. Keep in mind that your success and your institution's success are dependent upon building a successful relationship with the institution's president.

The VPs' varying approaches to change are set in the context of higher education at 10 highly respected doctoral-granting institutions, yet the complex decision-making landscape and significant challenges are familiar to many nonprofit advancement leaders. Do the challenges described in chapter 2 reflect issues in your own situation? Perhaps Jo's leadership vision is similar to yours and you, too, face the challenge of alumni disengagement. Follow how Jo approaches transforming her constituents.

Challenge 2 outlines significant questions critical to developing successful large gift strategies. This chapter could serve as the basis for a brainstorming session as part of a summer staff conference. Or these questions could help motivate flexible and creative large gift strategies adapted to your particular institution.

At a point in advancement history when many practitioners are searching for standard assessment criteria, Challenge 3 makes a strong case for finding both quantitative and qualitative criteria. The Advancement Constellation does not suggest you simply apply a solution to a challenge without regard to your own leadership vision. Instead it urges you to think about your style and your advancement landscape and to look for similar cases/solutions. It's not a one size fits all solution or approach.

The insights these 10 great leaders offer are deeply personal and without regard to their own public image. Use the candid advice section to mentor potential future advancement leaders and to remind yourself of ways to approach the challenges of your position. Share this with your human resource professionals to help guide mentoring and back-filling within the advancement organization.

Institution President

If you are an institution's president or dean or foundation director, you can use the Advancement Constellation in many ways. It can give guidance to your search for a new advancement leader. Often times, new institutional leaders come from academia and may not have direct experience leading an organization. In these cases, *Envisioning Advancement Leadership* can help shed light on the importance of a strong president–vice president relationship. Based on the advice of these 10 great advancement vice presidents, finding someone who you trust and who complements your strengths is critical. The section on the nuances of president–vice president relationship helps clarify the challenges you each face in approaching the complex advancement landscape.

Share this with your governing boards to help them understand the varying visions of institutional constituents, governance, and decision making. When board members understand the complexity of the environment, they may be able to provide increased support to the advancement vice president. Imagine a vice president facing Jo's challenge of increasing alumni support with a board that understands the numerous constituents she addresses versus a board that believes the alumni are her only audience.

Consider using the Advancement Constellation as a backdrop for a discussion with your executive team. Sometimes the chief financial officer doesn't see the relevancy of his or her interaction with the advancement leader. This book may shed light on the importance of the close working relationship of the entire senior team. Creating individual constituent maps and then comparing them across the senior team may uncover unspoken challenges related to sharing a common perspective on audience.

In these difficult economic times, being able to stand in the shoes of the advancement leader will enable the institutional president or dean or foundation director to attract greater funding and support.

Consultant

If you advise advancement leaders, the Advancement Constellation will help you structure conversations about the conundrums such leaders face. If you help institutions find new leaders, the Advancement Constellation provides a concise way to frame the search process. The framework provides a means to stimulate dialogue about the leadership needs of a given institution. In some situations, the university governing board may want the new leader to maintain the current campus culture and thus need a leader who can stay the course, whereas another university may need the new leader to radically change the way alumni relate to the university. To be successful, each of these situations requires a different type of leader. If you accept that "leadership is an interactive art" (Williams 2005), then you may see your job of coaching as a way to increase flexible and creative decision-making. In a world where advancement leaders seem to work 24/7, the Advancement Constellation offers the consultant coach a tangible method of assessing a particular leader's areas of expertise and areas for growth. Sometimes exploring fit is more easily done with the aid of an objective outsider rather than solely from one's personal perspective.

Academician

Whether you are teaching philanthropy, higher education administration, or nonprofit management, this book uses real-world examples to illustrate the advancement leader's decision-making process. While this work will not speak to the professor who teaches a particular leadership style, it does offer 10 coherent cases to the teacher who encourages a student to develop a personal leadership path.

The cases focus on leadership, but they are replete with the details of gathering support in higher education and offer the professor of philanthropy research on key issues in the field. The professor interested in investigating the multi-frame approach has enough information about each participant to suggest the student categorize each participant into one of the four frames. Conversely, the professor who wants to delve into the impact of political processes on decision making could use the composite map and the challenges to stimulate dialogue.

This work provides professors of qualitative research methodology sound examples of applying qualitative analysis. While qualitative research has been the fundamental instrument of some of the social sciences such as anthropology, there has been a strong focus on quantitative research methodologies in the recent past. Applying qualitative methodologies to investigate a practical problem offers the research professor an example that reveals the power of the methodology.

The student of any of these fields of interest will be able to have a virtual cup of coffee with some of the best advancement leaders in the business. One of the most challenging aspects of finding an individual career path is being able to envision the practical considerations and challenges. The real-life stories of the 10 participants provide an opportunity for the student to compare and contrast his or her views with some of the best in the field.

Finally, the researcher will find a springboard into deeper answers about the relationship of leadership, success, and organizational well-being. For example, this work suggests a deep connection between organizational culture and leadership decision-making. There is much left uncovered in the interviews that could help current and future advancement leaders tackle the shifting requirements of the culture challenge. Much of the existing research on leadership focuses on business or politics. Are the findings of Kotter (1996, 2002, 2008) and Pfeffer (1992, 2010) transferrable to the advancement landscape? Given the relevance of positive politics to the work of advancement, would a more extensive review of the work of Burns (1979, 2003, 2006) be beneficial? Much of the existing research on leadership in higher education has focused on the president (Duderstadt 2007; Fisher and Koch 2004; McLaughlin 1990, 1996, 2004). Chapter 1, "Recognizing the Cornerstones of Advancement Leadership," highlights several limitations to simply applying research on university presidents to advancement vice presidents. What additional research would be most helpful to advancement leaders?

In some ways this work asks as many questions as it attempts to answer. There is much room left to be explored. The bibliography and endnotes offer bread crumbs into future research possibilities.

Whether you are a practitioner or an academician, applying the Advancement Constellation provides a path to support those who strategically shape so many engines for good.

 CONCLUSION

Advancement leaders thoughtfully shape the future of their organizations. In the world of higher education, the path to success is full of ambiguity and difficult questions that don't have easy answers. Cohen and March reflect my admiration for the advancement leader:

> We believe that effective top executives are heroic; but their heroism lies not in their ability to lead their institutions to a pre-chosen destiny, not in their responsibility for the major successes and failures realized by their institutions, but in their willingness to try to do better in a world where neither the meaning of "better" nor the route to its realization is clear. (Cohen and March 1986, xvii)

Weaving together the participants' stories and existing leadership research, this study provides insights into how 10 advancement vice presidents have defined and exercised leadership. These snapshots capture valuable perspectives on this little-researched landscape. Rather than offer a one-size-fits-all prescription for advancement leadership practices, this study suggests a way of thinking about the nonprofit executive's vision of leadership, success, and organizational well-being.

FIGURE 1. The Advancement Constellation

Dynamic interaction argument

VP's vision of leadership and institutional environment dynamically interacts with his or her definition and approach to significant challenges

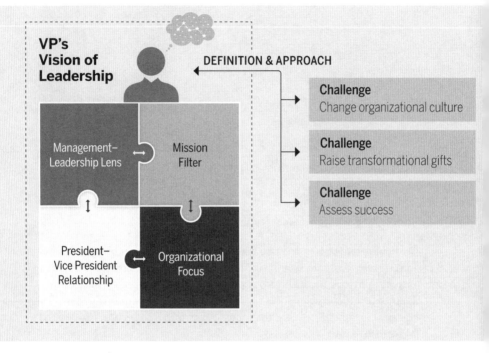

The Advancement Constellation illustrates how a participant's vantage point interacts with the VP's definition and approach to three common challenges. The diagram was repeated throughout the study to emphasize the importance of developing a holistic and multifaceted approach to understanding leadership.

Vantage Point: The Four Cornerstones Set in Place and Time

"Recognizing the Cornerstones of Advancement Leadership" demonstrates that a comprehensive grasp of advancement leadership requires examining the cornerstones of the VP's leadership theory: orientation of the management-leadership lens, particular view of mission, perspectives on the president–vice president relationship, and choice of organizational focus. The 10 participants share several common notions of leadership, represented in the diagram by the white space within the porous line. Yet it is the participants' differences that help clarify their vantage points. The way each participant resolves his or her perspective on managing versus leading forms the primary cornerstone. All the participants believe it is their mission to raise money, but some emphasize the importance of cultivating relationships in addition to seeking funds, and others focus on the need to tie funds to institutional priorities. In a similar way, the participants all note the importance of the vice president's relationship to the president. Yet the aspect each chooses to privilege helps clarify the individual vice president's vision of advancement leadership. Finally, the participant's choice of organizational focus reflects who the VP considers he or she is leading/managing and forms the final cornerstone of the participant's leadership theory. Chapter 1 establishes an advancement leadership framework as a means of understanding the complex decision-making landscape in which these nonprofit leaders function. Grasping the varying participant vantage points is the first step in understanding the interactivity of the model.

Dynamic Interaction of Vantage Point and Challenge

Chapter 2 exercises the Advancement Constellation in the context of the individual cases and shows how these VPs help institutions dream big dreams. This part makes evident how advancement leaders advocate for institutional strategic direction and plan ways to ensure that the institution's future is funded. Examination of the ways the participants address institutional culture and evaluate success in their work brings into play many concepts of governance, external factors, and the world of higher education administration. "Fitting Vantage Point with Challenge" uses concrete participant examples to show the value of investigating advancement leadership practices by looking at the dynamic interaction of each participant's leadership vision, advancement landscape, and challenge.

Leveraging Collective Wisdom

In chapter 3, an aggregation of the participants' insights is offered as advice to other practitioners who are developing their own leadership visions. Leveraging these VPs' insights and approaches is best done if it is absorbed with a strong dose of self-reflection. Based on the Advancement Constellation, it becomes evident that best practices and sage advice do not uniformly span diverse leadership theories and contexts.

Looking Ahead

Merging the model and the participants' collective wisdom suggests a practicing advancement leader make time to step outside his or her leadership vision, institution, and challenge to reflect on each from different angles. Leadership theorists (Bolman and Deal 2003; Heifetz 1994) propose that making such time will increase the decision maker's creativity and flexibility.

The Advancement Constellation emerged from research on leadership in complex organizations and an analysis of advancement vice presidents' perspectives on leadership, success, and organizational well-being. The model offers clarity to practicing advancement executives, to students wanting to understand one of the strategic senior leadership roles in nonprofit organizations, to researchers who want to use this study as a springboard to deeper research in this domain, and to any of the many philanthropists who devote themselves to making nonprofit work a powerful tool for good. Students of higher education leadership will read real-life quandaries and resolutions. Professors will find scholarly analysis of a little studied aspect of higher education leadership and will find qualitative research methodologies employed on a critical aspect of nonprofit leadership.

The protection of the vice presidents' anonymity offers the reader a rare opportunity to hear these advancement leaders' powerful insights in plain language, and the vice president does not risk the exposure of his or her institution, president, or donors. The model opens possibilities for sharpening and evolving a nonprofit advancement leader's development, decision making, institutional relationships, coaching practices, assessment strategies, best practice implementation strategies, organizational well-being, and recruitment strategies. Volunteers, university presidents, nonprofit board members, and others who work closely with advancement leaders will benefit from the clarity the model offers about this little-researched arena of advancement.

The advancement leader plays a strategic role in bringing together students seeking a brighter tomorrow, faculty whose ideas need funding, presidents and CEOs who want to propel their institutions into the future, alumni and friends who want to preserve or improve the quality of education, and donors who want to make a difference. The critical responsibility the advancement leader has in preserving and strengthening vital engines for improving the world at large calls for more extensive investigation into what does and doesn't work in pursuit of these worthy goals.

 BIBLIOGRAPHY

American Heritage College Dictionary. 2004. 4th ed. Boston: Houghton Mifflin.

Bennis, W. G., and B. Nanus. 2003. *Leaders: The Strategies for Taking Charge*. 2nd ed. New York: HarperCollins.

Bensimon, E. M. 1990. "The New President and Understanding the Campus as a Culture." *New Directions for Institutional Research* 68 (Winter): 75–86.

Bensimon, E. M., and A. Neumann. 1993. *Redesigning Collegiate Leadership: Teams and Teamwork in Higher Education*. Baltimore: John Hopkins University Press.

———. 2000. "What Teams Can Do: How Leaders Use—and Neglect to Use—Their Teams." In *Organization & Governance in Higher Education*, edited by M. C. Brown II, 244–57. Boston: Pearson Custom Publishing.

Birnbaum, R. 2004. "The End of Shared Governance: Looking Ahead or Looking Back." In *Restructuring Shared Governance in Higher Education*, edited by W. G. Tierney and V. M. Lechuga, 5–22. San Francisco: Jossey-Bass.

Bolman, L.G., and T. E. Deal. 2003. *Reframing Organizations: Artistry, Choice, and Leadership*. 3rd ed. Jossey-Bass Higher and Adult Education Series. San Francisco: Jossey-Bass.

Bongila, J.-P.K. 2003. *Funding Strategies for Institutional Advancement of Private Universities in the United States: Applications for African/Congolese Universities*. Boca Raton, FL: Universal-Publishers.

Booth, W. C. 2004. *The Rhetoric of Rhetoric: The Quest for Effective Communication*. Blackwell Manifestos. Malden, MA: Wiley-Blackwell.

Bornstein, R. 2008. "Presidents and the Big Picture." *Chronicle of Higher Education* 54 (40): A30.

Burdeno, M., and J. Herrmann. 2006. "Meet Newton North Principal Jennifer Price." City of Newton.

Burns, J. M. 1979. *Leadership*. New York: Harper & Row.

————. 2003. *Transforming Leadership: A New Pursuit of Happiness.* 1st ed. New York: Atlantic Monthly Press.

————. 2006. *Running Alone: Presidential Leadership from JFK to Bush II: Why It Has Failed and How We Can Fix It.* 1st ed. New York: Basic Books.

Cameron, K. S., and R. E. Quinn. 2011. *Diagnosing and Changing Organizational Culture: Based on the Competing Values Framework.* 3rd ed. Jossey-Bass Business & Management Series. San Francisco: Jossey-Bass.

Council for Advancement and Support of Education (CASE). 2012. "About Advancement." Accessed March 21. http://www.case.org/About_CASE/About_Advancement. html.

Council for Advancement and Support of Education (CASE) Career Central. 2012. Directory of Continuing and Graduate Education for Advancement Professionals. Accessed March 21. http://www.case.org/Career_Central/Directory_of_Continuing_ Education.html.

Council for Advancement and Support of Education (CASE) InfoCenter. 2008. Directory of Continuing and Graduate Education for Advancement Professionals.

Chaffee, E. E. 1987. "Organizational Concepts Underlying Governance and Administration." In *Key Resources on Higher Education Governance, Management, and Leadership: A Guide to the Literature,* edited by M. W. Peterson and L. A. Mets, 21–27. San Francisco: Jossey-Bass.

Cheever, D. 1982. "A Good Beginning as a Superintendent." In *Entry: The Hiring, Start-Up and Supervision of Administrators,* edited by B. Jentz and J. Woffard, 113–33. New York: McGraw Hill.

Clark, B. R. 1972. "The Organizational Saga in Higher Education." *Administrative Science Quarterly* 17 (2): 178–84.

Cohen, M. D., J.G. March, and Carnegie Commission on Higher Education. 1986. *Leadership and Ambiguity: The American College President.* 2nd ed. Boston: Harvard Business School Press.

DePree, M. 1989. *Leadership Is an Art.* New York: Dell.

Dill, D. D., and P. K. Fullagar. 1987. "Leadership and Administrative Style." In *Key Resources on Higher Education Governance, Management, and Leadership: A Guide to the Literature,* edited by M. W. Peterson and L. A. Mets, 390–99. San Francisco: Jossey-Bass.

Drozdowski, M. J. 2004. "A Matter of Degrees." *Chronicle of Higher Education* 50 (37): C2.

Duderstadt, J. J. 2007. *The View from the Helm: Leading the American University during an Era of Change.* Ann Arbor: University of Michigan Press.

Fisher, J. L., and J. V. Koch. 1996. *Presidential Leadership: Making a Difference.* Oryx Press Series on Higher Education. Phoenix: Oryx Press.

————. 2004. *The Entrepreneurial College President.* Westport, CT: Praeger.

French, J. R. P., and B. Raven.1986. "The Bases of Social Power." In *Political Leadership:*

A Source Book, edited by B. Kellerman, xv, 462. Pittsburgh: University of Pittsburgh Press, 1986.

Grunig, J. E., et al. 2000. "From Organizational Effectiveness to Relationship Indicators: Antecedents of Relationships, Public Relations Strategies, and Relationship Outcomes." In *Public Relations as Relationship Management: A Relational Approach to the Study and Practice of Public Relations,* edited by J. A. Ledingham and S. D. Burning, 23–53. Mahwah, NJ: Lawrence Erlbaum Associates.

Haden, W. 2000. "Boundaries of Leadership: The President and the Chief Advancement Officer." In *Handbook of Institutional Advancement,* edited by Peter McE. Buchanan. Washington, DC: CASE, 2000.

Heifetz, R. A. 1994. *Leadership without Easy Answers.* Cambridge, MA: Belknap Press of Harvard University Press.

Helsing, D., et al. 2008. "Putting the 'Development' in Professional Development: Understanding and Overturning Educational Leaders' Immunities to Change." *Harvard Educational Review* 78 (3): 437.

Hofstede, G. H., and G. J. Hofstede. 2005. *Cultures and Organizations: Software of the Mind.* 2nd ed., rev. and expanded. New York: McGraw-Hill.

Joslyn, H., J. C. Berkshire, and E. Quotah. 2009. "A Growing Leadership Gap." *Chronicle of Philanthropy* 21 (13): 29–31.

Julius, D. J., J. V. Baldridge, and J. Pfeffer. 1999. "A Memo from Machiavelli." *Journal of Higher Education* 70 (2): 113–33.

Keohane, N. O. 1985. "Collaboration and Leadership: Are They in Conflict?" *College Board Review* (135): 4–6.

Kotter, J. P. 1996. *Leading Change.* Boston: Harvard Business School Press.

———. 2002. *The Heart of Change: Real-Life Stories of How People Change Their Organizations.* Boston: Harvard Business School Publisher.

———. 2008. *A Sense of Urgency.* Boston: Harvard Business Press.

Madsen, H. 2002. *Literature Review of the Context for Leadership and Decision-Making in Higher Education: A Comparison to Government and the Corporate Sector, in Graduate School of Education.* Cambridge, MA: Harvard University.

———. 2004. *Institutional Decision-Making at Liberal Arts Colleges Led by Non-traditional Presidents.* Cambridge, MA: Harvard Graduate School of Education.

McLaughlin, J. B. 1996. "Leadership Transitions: The New College President." *New Directions for Higher Education, Number 93.* San Francisco: Jossey-Bass.

———. 2004. "Leadership amid Controversy: Presidential Perspectives." *New Directions for Higher Education, Number 128.* San Francisco: Jossey-Bass.

McLaughlin, J. B., and D. Riesman. 1990. *Choosing a College President: Opportunities and Constraints.* Special Report. Princeton, NJ: Carnegie Foundation for the Advancement of Teaching.

Michael, S. O., M. Schwartz, and L. Balraj. 2001. "Indicators of Presidential Effectiveness: A Study of Trustees of Higher Education Institutions." *International Journal of Educational Management* 15 (7): 332–46.

Mintzberg, H. 1990. "The Manager's Job: Folklore and Fact." *Harvard Business Review* 68 (2): 163–76.

A New Future for Education Funding in Economic Crisis Summit. 2008. Association of School Business Officials International.

Peterson, M. W., and L. A. Mets, eds. 1987. *Key Resources on Higher Education Governance, Management, and Leadership: A Guide to the Literature.* 1st ed. Jossey-Bass Higher Education Series. San Francisco: Jossey-Bass.

Pettigrew, A. M. 1977. "Strategy Formulation as a Political Process." *International Studies of Management & Organization* 7 (2): 78–87.

Pfeffer, J. 1992. *Managing with Power: Politics and Influence in Organizations.* Boston: Harvard Business School Press.

———. 2010. *Power: Why Some People Have It and Others Don't.* New York: HarperCollins.

Pusser, B. 2003. "Beyond Baldridge: Extending the Political Model of Higher Education Organization and Governance." *Educational Policy* 17 (121): 121–40.

———. 2005. "Arenas of Entrepeneurship: Where Nonprofit and For-Profit Institutions Compete." *New Directions for Higher Education, Number 120.* San Francisco: Jossey-Bass.

Pusser, B., and D. J. Doane. 2001. "Public Purpose and Private Enterprise." *Change* 33 (5): 18.

Rogers, C. R., and F. J. Roethlisberger. 1991. "Barriers and Gateways to Communication." *Harvard Business Review* 69 (6): 105–11.

Schiffrin, D. 2006. *In Other Words: Variation in Reference and Narrative.* Studies in Interactional Sociolinguistics 21. Cambridge, UK: Cambridge University Press.

"Three to Receive HAA Medal for Extraordinary Service." 2006. *Harvard University Gazette.*

Tierney, W. G., and V. M. Lechuga. 2004. "Restructuring Shared Governance in Higher Education." *New Directions for Higher Education, Number 127.* San Francisco: Jossey-Bass.

Tucker, R. C. 1995. "The Process of Political Leadership: Mobilizing Support." In *Politics as Leadership.* Columbia: University of Missouri Press.

Wheatley, M. J. 2006. *Leadership and the New Science: Discovering Order in a Chaotic World.* 2nd ed. San Francisco: Berrett-Koehler Publishers.

Williams, D. 2005. *Real Leadership: Helping People and Organizations Face Their Toughest Challenges.* San Francisco: Berret-Koehler.

INDEX

Note: Page numbers in *italics* indicate figures.

donor-institution tension, and
large gift strategies, 75
Drozdowski, M. J., 11
dynamic interaction of vantage
point and challenge. *See*
vantage point and challenge fit
dynamism, and Advancement
Constellation, 2, 46-47, 49-50

E

executives, and Advancement
Constellation, 95-96
external factors, and
organizational focus, 46-47

F

fundraising
advancement leadership and, 7
cornerstones of advancement
leadership and, 28, 31-32
president and, 32-33
. See also large gift strategies;
vantage point and challenge fit

G

gift plans, and large gift strategies,
73-75
Glimp, Fred, 11

H

Heifetz, R. A., 53

I

inherent complexity of institutions,
44-45
inspiration, 16
institutional attitude transformation, 58-60
institutional governance, 42, 45-46

institutional priorities, 26-27
integrity, 16, 17

K

knowledge about fit, 89-92

L

large gift strategies
about, 54, 71, 77-79, 78
achievement assessment and, 76
donor-institution tension and, 75
$100 million dollar gift story
and, 76-77
staff role and, 71-73
. See also fundraising; vantage
point and challenge fit
leadership lens
cornerstones of advancement
leadership and, 16-17
president and, 30-31
president-vice president
relationship and, 30-31
. See also management-leadership
lens
listening skills, 90, 93
long term focus, 28

M

management-leadership lens
cornerstones of advancement
leadership and, 3, 14-16
tension and, 20-25
management lens, 14-16, 17-19
management skills, 13
March, J. G., 44, 101
McLaughlin, J. B., 45-46
methodology, 1, 104
mission
assessment of success and, 82-83

cornerstones of advancement
leadership and, 3, 16, 26-29
modification of, 28-29

O

$100 million dollar gift story,
76-77
. See also large gift strategies
organizational focus
about, 3, 39, 47, *47*, *48*
composite constituent diagram
and, 42, *42*
constituents and, 39-40, *42*
external factors and, 46-47
inherent complexity of
institutions and, 44-45
institutional governance and,
42, 45-46
organization and, 39, 40-41, 44
prioritization of constituents
and, 42-44
stakeholders and, 40-41
vision of leadership and, *48*,
48-49
. See also cornerstones of
advancement leadership

P

partner development, 90, 92-93
passion, 90, 94
positive attitude, 16
preservation or changes in
organizational culture
about, 53-54, 55, 66-70, *70*
Advancement Constellation
and, 69-70
challenges described for, 55-58
institutional attitude
transformation and, 58-60

senior staff culture
transformation and, 60-66
. See also vantage point and
challenge fit
presidents of institutions, and
Advancement Constelltion, 97
. See also president-vice
president relationship
president-vice president relationship
about, 3, 30, 38, *38*
boss-employee relationship
and, 35-36
colleagues and, 34-35
fundraiser role of president
and, 32-33
leader role of president and,
30-31
leadership and, 30-31
team relationship and, 37
. See also cornerstones of
advancement leadership
Pusser, B., 44, 46

R

relationship building, 28-29
rhetoric described, 87

S

self knowledge about fit, 89-92
senior staff culture transformation,
60-66
sense of humor, 90, 94
service, 16
Spencer, Clayton, 46-47
staff
large gift strategies and, 71-73
senior staff culture transformation and, 60-66

stakeholders, and organizational
focus, 40-41

strategy, 16

T

team relationships, and president-
vice president relationship, 37

transformational gifts. *See* large
gift strategies

transformational leaders
described, 87

V

vantage point and challenge fit
about, 5-6, 53-54, 87-88, 103
Advancement Constellation
and, *84,* 85-87
rhetoric and, 87
transformational leaders and,
87
. *See also* assessment of success;
large gift strategies; preservation or changes in organizational culture

vision of leadership
assessment of success and,
82-83
cornerstones of advancement
leadership and, 16
organizational focus and, *48,*
48-49

 ABOUT CASE

The Council for Advancement and Support of Education (CASE) is a professional association serving educational institutions and the advancement professionals who work on their behalf in alumni relations, communications, development, marketing and allied areas.

Founded in 1974, CASE maintains headquarters in Washington, D.C., with offices in London, Singapore, and Mexico City. Its membership includes more than 3,600 colleges and universities, primary and secondary independent and international schools, and nonprofit organizations in nearly 80 countries. CASE serves more than 77,000 advancement professionals on the staffs of its member institutions and has more than 17,000 professional members on its roster.

CASE also offers a variety of advancement products and services, provides standards and an ethical framework for the profession, and works with other organizations to respond to public issues of concern while promoting the importance of education worldwide.